EQUINOX

E Q U I N O X

....

Life, love, and birds of prey

DAN O'BRIEN

LYONS & BURFORD, PUBLISHERS

Printed in the United States of America.

Design by Catherine Lau Hunt

10 9 8 7 6 5 4 3 2 1

Library of Congress Cataloging-in-Publication Data

O'Brien, Dan, 1947–
    Equinox : life, love, and birds of prey / Dan O'Brien.
        p.   cm.
    ISBN 1-55821-456-9
    1. Falconry—Great Plains—Anecdotes.   2. O'Brien, Dan, 1947–   .
I. Title.
SK321.024   1997
799.2′32′092—dc20
    [B]   96-41129
                                                                      CIP

for Kris

Hans Peters '46

CONTENTS

Author's Note

One of the challenges of writing a book about a somewhat obscure subject is to make the text clear enough to be understood by the average reader without insulting the aficionado. Over the centuries, falconry has developed its own jargon, and it is hard to guess what terms a person will be comfortable with. To help alleviate this problem, I have included a glossary at the end of the text, and introduced each term, in the margin, the first time it is used.

Time is something else that makes a book about falconry tricky. The pace of a good falconry season and the pace of a good book are not necessarily the same. I have taken some liberties with time in an effort to draw a good book from a good falconry season.

The falconry procedures and techniques here may not be the best approach to the sport. There are as many opinions on that as there are falconers. Even the definitions in the glossary might not be universally accepted. But I was more interested in writing a why-do book than a how-to book. There are other books for that, and I urge any beginner to read them all.

EQUINOX

Pre-
Season

*W*e were into the core of a Great Plains winter and the weather had driven most of us indoors. My wife, Kris, had been on call at the hospital the night before, so I'd spent the night at the ranch, where we keep the falcons, the dogs, a few horses, and a herd of cattle. In one corner of the old ranch house there is a room filled with books, and that is where I write. I try to get into that room and begin my work early, but that morning I sat in the kitchen sipping coffee, looking out the window, and checking the temperature every few minutes. For days the temperature had been lodged in the single digits below zero, but now, with the sky going a shade lighter, it was already four above.

There is no television in the ranch house. It is hard for a weak person to write books with a television in the house, so eight years ago I hauled the thing to the dump out behind the corral and replaced it with the gift Kris gave me for my fortieth birthday—a genuine, computerized, airport-grade, digital weather station. I watched the temperature ticking upward on the screen mounted on to the south wall of the kitchen. The wind was at six miles per hour from the northwest, the humidity was eighteen percent, the barometer was steady.

I moved to the sink and looked down at the chicken I'd taken out of the freezer the night before. It was one we had raised the summer before. It hadn't been plucked or gutted because falcons enjoy cleaning their own meals. I divided the chicken in two pieces and looked again out the window at the building dawn. My old setter, Spud, looked up from his place in front of the stove with the demeanor of a concerned, aging monarch. The young dogs, Melville and Moose, lay chewing on each other in the living room. They paid no attention to what was going on in the kitchen. They weren't old enough to feel my mood.

The wind was sharp and I pulled my jacket up around my neck on the way to the mews. Inside the building it was even colder.

MEWS. The place where falcons and hawks are housed.

The metal walls held the night's sub-zero temperature like a thermos bottle. I walked down the hall and opened the first door. Dundee, the tiercel peregrine falcon, stood on the high perch, puffed up like a feathered softball. When I laid the half chicken on another perch, he twisted his head upside down and eechipped softly. He came to the food before I left his chamber and I took a moment to watch him begin the depluming

TIERCEL. The male peregrine falcon; the male of any species of falcon.

EECHIP. A sharp, solicitous vocalization of a falcon, usually around the nest, which indicates contentment. It is often used as a greeting.

process. He was gentle and playful. The white chicken feathers flew into the cold air and floated to the frozen floor.

In the next chamber, Little Bird would not come down to her food. She had always been aloof with me; now she refused even to look my way. It was the off-season, and the birds would begin to molt soon. Little Bird, too, was puffed against the cold, and did not look deadly in the least. Her last flight of the year,

MOLT. A bird's annual change of feathers, usually in the spring and summer.

the month before, had been one of her best. I can recall every detail. A hundred yards into the winter wheat field a covey of Hungarian partridge had been digging in the snow to reach the tender shoots below. Little Bird left the fist with a wing beat strong from a season of flying. She climbed steadily into the wind. Up, up, up—a tiny speck in the pale blue sky. Spud and I waited until she had reached her pitch, perhaps a thousand feet above the frozen prairie. When I tapped Spud

PITCH. The height of a falcon as she waits on.

lightly on the back of the head, he charged ahead and ran straight for the partridge. By the time I had moved upwind of the partridge, Spud had pinned them down and stood rigid with his tail high. When I looked up, Little Bird was higher still.

Looking at her in her molting chamber it was hard to believe this was the same bird. She looked so benign now with one foot tucked up and her eyes relaxed and squinting through the vertical

STOOP. A falcon's dive from a height—sometimes a considerable height. There are a thousand different configurations of stoops and watching a good one unfold is arguably the most exciting part of game hawking.

STRIKE. To take off a falcon's hood. Also the first bay of a hound when it finds game.

bars of the chamber at the rising sun. It seemed impossible that this bird had rolled from her pitch high above the flushing partridge and flown straight down to intersect the lead bird with enough force to kill it dead in the air. But I knew it had happened. I could still hear the whistle of the stoop and the whop of the strike and I stood savoring the memory until the cold was well into my clothing.

When I got back to the house I jimmied another log into the stove and stood rubbing my hands in the rising heat. I thought about Kris just getting home to our house in Rapid City from a tough night at the hospital. She is an anesthesiologist and cold, slippery nights like the one just passed often produce lots of surgeries. She'd be lucky to get a couple of hours of sleep before she'd have to be back at the hospital for some meeting or another. It had been like this for ten years and I never understood how she did it. In spite of her overexposure to stressful work, we've lived a marvelous life so far—no children, some affluence in recent years, and exciting vacations when Kris gets a break. But work like Kris's takes a toll; smart doctors are always alert for signs of burnout. She was just ending a two-year stint as department chair during a time of upheaval in the medical community. Miraculously, she still loved her job. To keep it that way, she had decided to take a year's leave of absence. That morning at the ranch I was watching the weather and thinking about the year to come. How my thoughts drifted from the pale gray sky and Kris's need for a break to fishing I'm only now beginning to understand.

In the finest tradition of writers, I was allowing, even encouraging, any thought to come into my mind as an alternative to going into my office and writing. Spud stared into the fire and I figured he must be doing something similar. I loved that idea. It occurred to me, then, that there are two kinds of people in the world: those who have caught a fish and those who have not.

Fishing? The lakes and streams for five hundred miles had been frozen for months. Maybe it was the sheer impossibility of it that got me thinking about fishing. Maybe it was my usual dread of sitting down in front of the word processor. Maybe it was a simple longing to be somewhere warm with a fly rod in my hand. I stared out the window and wondered if there would be a seam on the horizon that day or if the sky would continue to blend quietly into the snowscape.

I wasn't sure why I was uneasy. Could it be the weather or a change in barometric pressure that was bothering me? I looked up to the weather station. The barometer was still steady. No, it wasn't the weather and it wasn't simply the uncertainty of the year ahead: Worry about the future had never been a major bugaboo for me. Maybe it was that I'd turn forty-eight in that year and, just then, that seemed pretty old.

But my mind kept coming back to fishing. It made sense to me that the world can be divided into those who have and those who haven't. It isn't exactly catching fish that makes the difference. It isn't, as some say, the fulfillment of a desire to possess them—I'd only killed a handful of fish in the last fifteen years. No, there's something else. I stood up in the kitchen and mimicked a cast. Spud turned from the fire and looked squarely into my eyes—something dogs are not supposed to do—saw what I was doing and turned back to the fire. I went back to fishing. I mended twice and, when my fly floated over the brown trout rising behind the refrigerator, I gently raised the rod tip and there, right there, I understood part of what was puzzling me.

It is the quiver of another life that makes the difference, the feel of it through an instrument as delicate as nerve endings.

Once I asked a famous American fisherman to explain the technique he used to fight a trophy fish. He shrugged and said, "You just have to stay attached." Then he shook his head. He wasn't really sure how he landed all those lunkers and he felt he wasn't getting his meaning across. But I understood. What he meant is, however it's done, staying attached is all that's really important.

Remembering this, I saw what had been unsettling me since early in the morning when the dogs had burrowed under my blanket and eased me awake with soft, warm muzzles. Before she left for the hospital two days before, Kris had received a call from Dartmouth Medical School. She had been awarded a fellowship to study critical care medicine. The appointment would begin in July and last an entire year. I was worried about the ranch, the dogs, the falcons. I was worried about how I would stay attached.

I sat down at the oak table and looked out the patio doors, over the deck, and down the woody draw that drains into the stock pond where thick rainbows cruised cool and silent under the ice. I was on fishing again and the black rainbow backs in our pond reminded me of permit, the gigantic, supercharged panfish of the tropics.

Permit can slip out of the deep blue water, over the reef, and onto the tidal flats with a speed that causes a fisherman to wonder if he is hallucinating. They are relatively rare on the flats; their beauty—the graceful jet black line, sickle tail, and blues bleeding to buff—is profound. Their strength is legendary. A cross between a manhole cover and a torpedo, they are extremely hard to catch. When the choice of equipment is a fly rod, the difficulty approaches that of unicorn photography.

There are endless stories of men and women spending years, and who knows how much money, in pursuit of permit. Just to get a permit to follow a meticulously tied crab-fly is considered a feat; almost no one has ever caught more than a few. I have been present for only one successful encounter. It was off the coast of Belize on an open flat with no coral or mangroves to ruin things. My partner, Marshall Cutchin, was on the casting deck and we all knew that if he hooked a fish he had an excellent chance of landing it. For most fishermen it would have been the chance of a lifetime. That's why it struck me as odd that, when he did hook a fish, he chose to fight it with his eyes closed.

We had been searching for permit for five days. We had fished in wind, rain, and stagnant heat. We had seen a few fish, cast to a couple, but never connected. On the final day of the trip there it was, the black scimitar tail slicing reflected clouds through the tide and back toward the distant mangroves. The line was cleared and checked as the guide began poling the skiff to intercept the zigzagging wake. It was an excruciatingly slow stalk with Marshall's toes radaring the waves as they fondled the line coiled on the casting deck. The pole slipped through the water silently, but clumsily compared to the permit tail. There was a hint of blue in the tail now as it cut the water like a scalpel. Then, the reflection of clouds scudded on and there was the fish, preposterously beautiful. A beat. Then the exquisite back cast. Shoot a little line. Again. Farther. The line rolling into the wind and time slowing as the fly turned over, entered the water, and began its skittering descent. Time slowed still more. Then, as the fish turned, the world seemed to stop completely.

For me, with the flash of the permit's side, things clicked back into full speed. There was a swirl, the rod tip came up. Tight.

Marshall was attached. There was a long critical second as we watched the extra line crackle like electricity through the guides. When it went tight, the reel began instantly to hiss. First the line, then the backing, began to melt like spring snow. I was whooping and hollering, shouting advice faster than the guide. The boat seemed frantic with activity until I realized that only the guide and I were frantic. Marshall was calm, eyes closed as if he were taking a beautiful woman into his arms. He was swaying and palmed the reel as gently as you would touch a sleeping child. He smiled as though he could hear cello music, but he kept the rod tip high. When the fish went left, he tilted the rod right. When the fish went right, he tilted left. When the fish allowed it, he reeled. When it wouldn't, he let it run. It took over twenty minutes to bring that permit to the boat and in all that time Marshall never opened his eyes, never uttered a word, never changed expression.

To understand what that afternoon in Belize meant, you need to know that Marshall is a Key West fishing guide—very experienced—making his living helping others find and catch permit. But the day I was with him, he was on vacation—a busman's holiday, a chance to feel for himself the life he knows so much about, pulsing at the end of two hundred feet of line. But there's more. This guy graduated from Tufts University and did a graduate program at Harvard. He worked in publishing in Philadelphia, Princeton, and Washington, D.C. He bagged it all to become a Keys guide, to stay as close as possible to the thing he loves most.

There is no way to know what was going through Marshall's mind during the twenty-one minutes it took to land the fish, but I've come to believe that he was only thinking about staying attached, soaking every turn and head shake into himself, savoring every second.

Everyone who has seen a permit has fallen in love. It is impossible not to flirt with the idea of pursuing that brand of total attachment for yourself. But it's also beyond the knowledge, resources, and skills of most of us. It takes a lifetime to know an animal and its habitat that well.

It was a comfort to me that winter morning to know that, like Marshall, I too had a ground wire to reality. The dogs were part of it. The falcons in the mews were part. The prairie that surrounds the house was part. I looked through the sliding glass door and, as if on command, a trio of sharp-tailed grouse sliced the milky sky. Spud came to his feet and I laid my hand on his back. I wasn't sure what would happen in the year to come but I knew staying attached was everything.

When Kris first told me she was thinking about taking a year off work I imagined the two of us traveling for a couple of months through Europe in search of great food. I thought of fishing in Argentina. I had visions of Caribbean islands. But in my mind, all of these activities would take place between January and June. From the beginning, I imagined that Kris and I would spend the autumn on the prairie, flying falcons at ducks, partridge, and, above all, sharp-tailed grouse. Who would have thought she'd choose a year in congested New England, caring for very sick people six days a week and being on call every other night?

Her decision was a little like an Army colonel deciding to take some time off to rejuvenate himself by going back to boot camp.

The concept of every other night on call in a critical care unit needs some explaining. This is not like being on call for a cab company. This is not, "If they have trouble at the office they're going to give me a call." This is signing on to sleep only three or four nights a week for a year. This is being responsible for a dozen people who are almost dead and are plugged into machines that cost as much as B-1 bombers. This did not sound like a year off to me.

A few months before she heard from Dartmouth I had bemoaned to Kris that even though I hunted, fished, and flew falcons every fall, it was always a part-time endeavor. I was driving back and forth from Rapid City. I was working on a book. I never felt I'd given the effort everything I could. Deep down I suspected that was the reason for occasional lukewarm performances by dogs and falcons. My dream, I had told her, was to spend three months focused entirely on trying to do falconry right, completely folding myself into the rhythms of the animals. The months surrounding the autumn equinox are prime time for such a venture and so I had come to think of the scheme as my equinox dream. If you figured it a certain way, I was easily three-quarters of the way through my life, as the fall equinox is three-quarters of the way through the year. I saw myself approaching the autumnal equinox of my existence. It seemed high time for testing my fantasies.

But the planned year in Dartmouth changed all that. Kris and I have always supported each other; now it was my turn. She had just nursed me through two years of self-doubt and her efforts had produced a novel that I had thought I couldn't write. I owed her one.

Before I knew it, spring had come. Leaves were forcing themselves from the cottonwood buds. Even though I knew going to

New Hampshire would spoil my plans to hack a new falcon and fly her and the intermewed birds seriously in the fall, I bucked up one day and told Kris I thought it was a great idea for us to spend a year away from the ranch. Ducks had begun to arrive from their wintering grounds and Kris knew I'd spent most of the afternoon walking in the pastures of the ranch. She looked at me like I was crazy. "You can't spend the fall away from here," she said. "You've got baby falcons coming. You have dogs that are depending on you." Now she was kidding me. "Come out to New Hampshire after Thanksgiving. This is your chance to make your equinox dream come true."

HACK. To release falcons or hawks into the wild temporarily to allow them to develop their powers of flight and emotional maturity more naturally; to release into the wild permanently.

INTERMEW. To keep a bird of prey through a molt.

At first I was a little hurt. I'd have liked her to say that she needed me out there in New England. But she pointed out that I was between projects, that it was a perfect time for me to spend a few months doing just what I always wanted to do. It would be nice if I'd help her move but other than that she didn't expect to see me until we met in New Brunswick in October for our annual woodcock hunt. I could make it back to South Dakota in time for the last couple of weeks of the duck season and then get serious about grouse.

It was true that I had already arranged for a clutch of peregrine falcons to hack at the ranch. Releasing the birds, letting them learn to fly and hunt on their own, then trapping them back is not a simple undertaking. It requires a lot of time and wasn't something I

CLUTCH. A group of eggs or young birds, usually from a single nesting effort of a pair of adults.

could do if I planned to be in New Hampshire for the fall. There were also a couple of jobs I had been putting off for a year or so—a little building to put up at the ranch and a hundred small improvements.

I had a good stable of dogs. All the stock ponds were full so there were plenty of breeding ducks. There had been a considerable number of male grouse on the dancing grounds, so that population promised to be good too. It would be a shame to be incarcerated in New England while such a potentially glorious autumn wasted away on the Great Plains.

The more I thought about it, the more irresistible it seemed. Little Bird and Dundee had never reached their full potential, probably because I was always being torn away from working with them at critical times. If I had four months to work with them, I was sure that Little Bird could learn to be more consistent

QUARRY. The particular game pursued by a falcon or hawk.

in her flying and more tenacious with difficult quarry. With my undivided attention and effort, Dundee might be able to catch doves with some degree of style.

But I didn't feel right letting Kris go off on her own while I spent my time in adult play, so the decision languished. I couldn't put it off for much longer, however, because in late June, Pete Jenny, a

HACKBOX. The home of hack falcons or hawks in the week before release and the place where they are fed until they are taken up for training.

friend in Sheridan, Wyoming, would have three nestling peregrines ready to put in the hackbox at the ranch. He wanted one bird back to fly, and we figured of the three, one would decide to migrate. The third one would be for me. If I accepted the

birds, I would be committed and Kris would be destined to spend the first four months of her fellowship alone.

Like most lives, mine often seems a tangle of contradictions. If there is any consistency, for me it's always been a love affair with a certain class of wild things: falcons, their prey, and the prairie where I live. My anchor has been falconry. It is not merely sport; it is a lifestyle. Long ago I chose it because it is full of challenge and surprise and, in its purest form, completely untouched by the hobgoblins of almost all other aspects of twentieth-century life. In its purest form, falconry has no product—certainly it is not the game that is caught—it is all process. It is a chance to be part of something big and vital but void of ego and avidity. There is no better point of entry into the natural world than falconry. It forces you to see what cannot be put into books or taught in a classroom. In the best falconry there is no competition, no score, no end—just a web of activity, trailing on to infinity. It is an ideal that is seldom achieved but worth the effort.

For decades I'd made decisions that kept me grounded in a life from which most have been insulated for at least a generation. The ranch house, the dogs, the morning free to think, the constant sky, all are testament to those decisions. With all the modern pressures to do otherwise, it hasn't been easy. My deepest desire, to give over to it completely, has been constrained by my pesky connection to the civilized world. I've found society has trouble with those who lean toward the path of Conrad's Kurtz. But I've always had an attraction for that path and, with the possible exception of Kris, that has made the people closest to me uneasy.

My father might have had a disturbing inkling when I was caught skipping school to walk the flood-swollen riverbanks of Northwestern Ohio. If I had been a little older he would have understood playing hooky to drink beer, go to a Cleveland Indians game, or chase girls. But I was only twelve, and when I told him I was

HAWK. Strictly speaking these are accipiters—short-winged hawks—but the term can also refer to buteos and even falcons used in the sport of falconry.

walking the Blanchard River to see what the flood had done to the hickory trees where the red-tailed hawks nested, he shook his head. It was hard for him to conceive of a healthy boy so concerned about such things. Walking in the rain and mud? What could be gained?

I'll never forget my father's head shake. (He would give a similar shake when I told him I planned to be a writer.) Because I loved and respected him, I feared that he thought I was making a mistake, that I was wasting my life. It turns out that he didn't think that at all. In fact, he encouraged me much the way Kris encourages me now. But I'm sure he never quite understood and I've always wondered what he really thought.

It's been over thirty-five years since that wet Ohio spring and nothing much has changed. I never got a degree that was worth much in economic terms. I never worked a permanent job with a future. I never made a great business decision. What I have are degrees in literature, twenty years of working in the wind, a mortgage on a little ranch in South Dakota on which every previous owner has gone broke. Still, I've learned a few things.

I learned that that Ohio flood had no perceivable effect on the red-tailed hawks' nesting success. They raised three young that year and I screwed up my courage enough to climb the shagbark hickory and bring one to earth in a wicker basket. I named that first bird Agnes. Once she fledged, she developed an odd habit of sitting for hours on the telephone pole facing the neighbors' yard. I was learning to be a falconer the hard way. There were no mentors back then. Books were old, English, and hard to come by. It was mostly trial and error. I had no idea that keeping a bird loose and training it at the same time is nearly impossible. I had been cutting Agnes's weight down, trying to get her to chase rabbits. That was the right thing to do. But it was wrong to give her liberty while this lowering of weight was under way.

One afternoon, she flew to her usual place on the pole over the alley but only stayed there for an instant. She bailed off the other side as if she'd been shot and for an awful moment I thought she had been. I ran to the fence separating our yard from the neighbors' and there were

MANTLE. A hunched, drooped wing posture of falcons and hawks. Often used to protect a kill or the lure. Also a comfort movement in birds, to stretch a wing and leg on the same side at the same time.

Billy and Jane Mustard, both a couple of years younger than I was, leaning over my mantling redtail. I had no idea what they were doing until the redtail bucked into the air and the Mustards' pet duck, Donald, quaked and began flapping in a death spasm.

It was a neighborhood crisis in which the true colors of the combatants were revealed. The Mustard children would have gone to trauma therapy had there been such a thing back then. Their father, Arnold Mustard, became militant even though it was well known that, for fecal outrages of his patio, he was ready to kill Donald himself. And my father, bless his heart, became protective of me and quite amused by the whole affair. I remember the final confrontation over the backyard fence.

"That bird's vicious," Mr. Mustard sputtered. "It should be put to sleep."

"He was just doing what he was made to do," my father said.

"Donald was part of our family. We've had him since Easter. The kids are devastated."

"I know how you must feel, Arnold. I'll buy you a new duck."

"No, no."

"Hell, I'll buy you two new ducks."

"No. You can't make up for what's happened."

"Well, let me try," my father said to a retreating Mr. Mustard. "I'll get you a goose," he called across the yard. "How about two ducks and a goose?"

After the incident, except when I took her out in the country, that first redtail was confined to quarters. I kept her for a couple of years and eventually caught a few rabbits with her at the city dump. And every year since that time there has been at least one bird of prey in my mews.

The facility has evolved over the years, from a tiny lean-to built of packing crates on the side of my grandmother's house to a steel building with summer and winter quarters and a separate weathering yard, our current setup. In the metal building there is a mouseproof closet filled with telemetry equipment, electric collars, hardwood falcon blocks, check cords, and bath pans. There are postal scales for weighing the birds along with dozens of hoods, any one of which I would have killed for at age twelve.

Our kennel is modest, mostly because the dogs don't spend much time in it. For falconry—and I suspect for most hunting—it's more important that the dogs like you and have a chance to develop their canine powers for mind reading than it is to have the focus generated by a kennel life. Gundogs have numerous opportunities to make mistakes, but their mis-

WEATHERING YARD. An area where falcons and hawks are weathered. Federal regulations rightly dictate that a weathering yard should be a wire enclosure with a windbreak to ensure that the birds are safe from predators and protected from severe weather.

BLOCK. A cylinder, usually of laminated wood, staked to the ground and used by falcons as a perch while weathering.

HOOD. The sometimes exquisitely made leather cap that covers a falcon's head and eyes. Used to keep the falcon calm and safe before flying or in potentially frightening situations; the act of putting the hood on the falcon.

takes seem less important. If they bump a bird or fail to find a bird that you know is there, no real damage is done. You can simply keep on hunting until they get it right. But falconry dogs can be in trouble before they get out of the truck. One mistake and the whole day can be spoiled. A falcon's training depends on good dog work. Failure or bad behavior can result in ruined or lost falcons. The whole show depends on dogs knowing exactly what is expected, and there's no way to train them to know their place in every situation. They have to be able to figure things out, and lying around the house, studying their people's bizarre behavior, seems to help. For this reason, our dogs spend most nights in either the Rapid City house or the ranch house. The senior dog (presently Spud) has full-time house privileges. The rest of the pack goes out to the two runs built on the side of the barn when Erney, our caretaker and friend, goes outside to do the chores each morning.

Erney lives in his own little log cabin fifty yards east of the house. He uses the kitchen in the house and usually has the coffee going by the time I show up from Rapid City. If I stay at the ranch, the coffee is perking by the time he comes over from his cabin. We sit and drink at least a pot while we talk about the news, the weather, the day ahead.

They quit making people like Erney in about nineteen twenty-two. He's a throwback, a second-generation American of Czech descent who grew up in a South Dakota community that prides itself on being Bohemian. There was no plumbing in his childhood house, no insulation in the walls. The first language he heard was Czech.

His father died when Erney was very young, leaving his mother to raise the six kids any way she could. One of the family jobs was cleaning ducks, geese, and chickens for the local grocery store and pheasants for out-of-state hunters. Those were the days of six-bird limits with one hen, and the whole family was kept busy for weeks. Erney has probably cleaned more pheasants than everyone else I know combined. His mother saved the feathers from ducks and geese in huge sacks to be brought out on nights when winter held the family prisoner in the tiny house. They would eat popcorn, listen to the radio, and strip the down from feather shafts to make pillows and comforters. I've seen some of the comforters his mother made and have no trouble believing Erney's stories of waking up snug and warm, even with frost covering everything in the kids' unheated bedroom.

Growing up like this gives a person an earthiness that is rare these days. When it comes to self-reliance, Erney makes Emerson look like a piker. He's a confirmed bachelor who can live on thin air. A little venison, maybe a chicken or two, a bag of apples, a couple of cords of wood and he's good for the winter. In many ways Erney is a hermit, but occasionally he is gregarious. He raises orchids and fancy chickens. Though he doesn't fish, he ties hundreds of dozens of flies for the local fly shop (no doubt a holdover from all those childhood nights playing with feathers). He relishes hosting visitors and more than once I have felt left out while Erney chatted up a European guest or a well-known writer. Everyone likes Erney. People seem to look beyond his eccentricities and self-described status as a "world-class slob" to appreciate the kind and gentle person he is.

But Erney can be an irascible old bastard, too. He has no time for the acquisitive appetites of modern America, religion, and authority in general. He hates politicians, yuppies, and preachers and he tends to pity people who don't know the Latin names of common plants.

Erney came to work for me eleven years ago. Those were tough times. It was before Kris and I got together. Cattle prices were low, interest rates high, and I couldn't make the land payments. The same week that I determined I had to leave South Dakota for a construction job in California, Erney called to say the farm where he'd been working had gone broke. It was one of those divine interventions. We had lived together years before, when I was in graduate school and he was working for the state highway department. We were drawn together by our love for falconry, and that remains a driving force in our relationship. When he first came to the ranch, he was almost forty-five years old and crippled in one leg. About the only thing he had to show for all his years of farmwork was a missing thumb, the result of a glove hooking in the power takeoff of a tractor. He was way down on his luck, and my luck wasn't much either.

He showed up with thirty-eight dollars in his pocket and all his belongings in the back of a junk pickup truck. I was tickled and relieved to see him. I'd had to sell off the cows to make the last payment, but there were falcons in the mews and Erney is a solid falconer. He could take care of them and make sure things didn't fall apart while I was gone. In the spring he could put up hay while I sent paychecks home to the ranch. It was a match made in heaven. He was pleased to have a place and gladly took the lonely job of caretaker/falconer. I was just happy I didn't have to turn the ranch back to the bank.

Erney has a few more miles on him now. He's only in his middle fifties but he could pass for seventy. The bad leg has gotten to the point where he can only be on it a few hours a day. When he walks, it bows terribly at the knee. He once suggested welding up a leg brace in our shop to keep the thing from buckling on him. I didn't think it was such a good idea. But the attitude illustrated by his willingness to build his own prosthesis is basic to Erney's personality. I have known many people who fancy themselves free of the restraints of society. I know artists, businessmen, professors, and those of independent means who have orchestrated their lives for maximum autonomy. But when it comes to freedom from the daily demands of life, none of these people is in Erney's league. His secret for achieving a hassle-free life is simple: Don't do anything you don't want to do. If lines at the Division of Motor Vehicles bother you, drive without a license. Problems with the IRS? Don't file. Boss has a dumb idea? Ignore it.

Erney's bullheadedness runs deep, but it's completely without malice. He doesn't complain and stick his chin out. He simply doesn't do what he doesn't want to do. A perfect example of this is his response to my request to clean up after himself. Erney has a certain pride in being a slob. He proclaims it in his gentle way: "I was never one to mind a mess." He was also never one to clean up a mess.

Because we fix and build a lot of things, our workshop is reasonably well equipped. We have a couple of welders, a cutting torch, table saw, drill press, hand tools for most jobs, and all the specialized tools needed for ranching. Few days go by that one of us doesn't spend time in the shop. Some of our projects—fixing our junk baler, building a hackbox for the falcons, remodeling the inside of the stock trailer, constructing a deck on the side of the house—leave the shop a terrific mess. I'm of the belief that the job isn't done until it's cleaned up. But for putting tools away Erney accuses me of being anal-retentive. In all fairness, I have to say that Erney has a great memory for where he leaves tools. "The sledge? Did you try the back of the brown pickup?" "Big Phillips screwdriver? I think I used it in the well pit." He's usually right but it takes a long time to collect things before you start the next job, and ever since Erney came to the ranch I've been trying to get him to clean up the shop.

A few years ago it got so bad that I felt something had to be done. I told Erney he should clean the shop up once a month. He said that sounded like a good idea and he'd try. But a couple of months went by and nothing happened. There were three inches of sawdust on the floor, tools were scattered, I couldn't find anything. We talked about it again and he admitted it was a mess. I hated to put my foot down but felt I had to. "Okay," I said, "every first of the month I'm going to check the shop and if it's reasonable, I'll give you your paycheck. If it's a mess I'll hold it until you get things picked up."

I felt silly and somewhat draconian withholding his pay. He doesn't get much, and it's all he has to live on. But he agreed that I was being fair. After all, I wasn't asking for a Herculean effort, just a clean shop. He admitted he'd been lax and that he should do better. But he never said he *would* do better.

The first of the month came and I took a look at the shop. The sawdust was even deeper, so I brought it to Erney's attention and held his little check. Erney said he'd get around to the shop "one of these first days." The next month nothing had changed. Erney was still cheerful and joked that he'd been pretty busy. I held his second check.

I don't know what the guy ate for the next four months but my conscience finally forced me to relent. In the end, I just clipped the checks together, put them on the kitchen counter where he'd find them, and went out to clean the shop myself. That was in nineteen ninety-two and I still can't find a hammer when I need one.

Erney and I have known each other for over twenty-five years. Though we see the world in different ways, we're the best of friends, and our passions are very much the same. Central in our lives is hunting with falcons, and our lives mesh in such a way that we are able to run a better-than-average falconry establishment. Since Erney isn't very mobile, he's not one for chasing a dog down or running to the top of a hill to see where the falcon went. He doesn't like to make the hunting trips that are necessary in years of low game numbers. He isn't much for making the demands on the birds that bring them to true hunting pitch. But he is very steady and has enormous patience. He is the best I have ever seen at taming wild falcons, a master of the art of manning birds of prey, and can work the birds when I'm off doing something to make a living.

MAN. To tame by prolonged and intimate exposure to people and the human world.

Our passion for falconry is emblematic of our interest in wildlife ecosystems, and we're lucky enough to have a laboratory in which to pursue that interest. Our ranch is located on the western edge of South Dakota, twenty miles from Wyoming, thirty-five from the Montana line. The Black Hills take up the southern horizon; to the southeast, Bear Butte rises a thousand feet from the prairie floor. It is not a big ranch by South Dakota standards. It's eleven hundred acres of brushy draws and grassy flats that run northeast from the house. A mile-and-a-quarter-long driveway empties into the homestead where three outbuildings—the homing pigeon loft, the mews/workshop, the horse barn—shelter the house from the northwest wind. The house is old and has only six rooms, but we've added lots of windows, so great sweeps of the ranch are visible in every direction. From the living room I can keep an eye on a whole section of pastureland. When the cattle are grazing I can check on them with binoculars from the deck on the east side of the house. A mile farther east is a few hundred acres of marginal farmland that we cut hay from in the good years, but our place is best suited for cattle grazing. In the seventies and early eighties, before Kris and I met, before I sold my first book, before Erney came to work, I ran a herd of sixty mother cows. The place was what is known as a cow-calf operation. That means I took care of the mother cows all year long. In winter I fed them the hay I had put up the summer before. In spring I helped them have their calves; in fall I sold the calves. The calves were the only cash crop in those days, and because all the money was borrowed and interest rates were high, they never brought enough to make a living. To make ends meet, I took jobs with wildlife agencies or on other ranches. As we say in South Dakota, I worked out.

Now the mother cows are gone and we're called a yearling operation. According to the market, we buy between one hundred and one hundred fifty steers or heifers sometime between December and May. They weigh about five hundred pounds when they come off the trucks. We put them in our feedlot and try to put fifty pounds on them by serving up last summer's hay. When the grass turns green in May they go out to pasture, where we hope they'll gain another two hundred pounds. We sell them in August, before the pastures are grazed down. The profit—when there is any—is in the pounds they gain. It is not a coincidence that the ranch is free of cattle between August and December. Those months are too precious to waste taking care of them, and the grass we so carefully conserve during the summer is too precious simply to let cattle eat.

On the Great Plains, grass is everything. Everything that creeps or crawls or flies or drives a pickup owes its existence to grass. The health of that existence depends on the health of the grass and most of the grass on the Great Plains is not that healthy. Our ranch and a few ranches that neighbor us form a small island in an ocean of generally devastated land. Most people would only notice the difference in dry years when the overgrazed land is obviously short of grass. But it's not the height of the grass that's important. It is the population of plants that tells the story.

It has taken eighteen years to bring our pastures back to near health. Now little bluestem, western wheat grass, and grama grass are coming back into the areas where cattle—because they like the taste of it—brought it to the edge of extinction. Some people don't know that grass makes up ninety-nine percent of a cow's diet. Many think the major product of the Great Plains is beef, but it's not. The major product of the Great Plains is grass. Cows are just a way to harvest the grass, just a way to get it to market. This ignorance is not confined to city dwellers; there are many ranchers who know very little about grass, too. They can only identify a few species when there are hundreds in their pastures, each with unique characteristics, each with a different value as livestock forage, soil stabilizer, and wildlife habitat. The grass on the Great Plains has been abused for a century—not so much by greed as by ignorance.

It is impossible to judge the condition of rangeland by looking out over it. From a distance dying range looks very much like healthy range. It's only when the abuse is acute that the difference can be discerned from the cab of a pickup. To tell what is happening in a pasture, you have to get out into it. You have to get on your hands and knees and touch things. You have to know what you're looking at, and that's not easy.

A pasture changes almost daily. The growth of certain cool-season grasses might be slowing as some warm-season grasses begin to flourish. Insects come and go. Weeds and exotic grasses take advantage of every opportunity to thrive. But the two main agents of pasture change are weather and grazing. No one can do anything about the weather, but grazing pressure, frequency, and timing can be regulated if a rancher has the ambition to learn about the dynamics.

The main obstacle to good grazing practices seems to be tradition. For example, over most of the West, herds are moved onto pastures at almost exactly the same time each year and later moved off on almost exactly the same day. This could mean that for eighty years there have been two hundred head of cows and calves on a given pasture between June first and September fifteenth. This might mean that for eighty years cattle have feasted on warm-season grasses from the time the plants begin to grow in the spring until they go dormant in the fall. These species have been put under great pressure and seldom have the chance to develop seed heads and reproduce normally. Eventually, these grasses begin to die out and less palatable vegetation begins to take their place. If this goes on for too long, the best grasses cease to exist in that pasture. The better grazing grasses are always harder hit because they are the varieties cattle prefer. As the favorite species begin to thin, the value and vitality of the pasture are diminished. Then the cattle move on to their second favorite species and so on, until the pasture is a very different ecosystem from the one the first cattle rancher found when he brought his herd up from Texas in the late nineteenth century.

Unfortunately, this process is gradual and nearly impossible to perceive. Only when families experience a decline in beef production do they suspect that something is wrong. By then, of course, the pasture is severely damaged and has long since ceased to support native wildlife.

The ability to understand what is really happening is rare. It's a question of serious training, not, as many suggest, a matter of common sense. In fact, contrary to popular belief, "common sense" can lead to all sorts of wrongheaded conclusions. (Erney drove this point home one morning when talking about computers. "Common sense," he said, "would tell you that a machine that can only count to one can't be worth much.")

On our ranch we try to know all we can about grasses, what they need, when they are healthy, how much and when they should be grazed. But to do it right would take at least a doctorate in agronomy. Improving pasture is very difficult. It's expensive, technical, and a lot of work. Figuring out if what you're doing is having any effect can also be tough. One way a rancher could find out if his management techniques are producing results is to commission a rangeland expert to study his ranch for several years. The other way to find out how he's doing is to commission a whole flock of rangeland experts.

We've taken the second option. If we want to know the condition of our pastures, we go for a walk with a bird dog and count sharp-tailed grouse. It's not the absolute number that's important in determining the health of a pasture; the number depends mostly on yearly weather patterns. But the number of grouse in a given pasture relative to that of the pasture next door tells most of the story. Grouse will use the healthiest range they can find. They're right down in it every day and are sensitive to nuances we can only imagine. They are better range evaluators than the most learned of scientists. Where there are grouse there are fat cattle—and usually plenty of other species of wildlife, from deer to dung beetles.

We concentrate on making our ranch the preferred home of all the sharp-tailed grouse in our township for two reasons. First, their presence proves that our pastures are healthy; second, they are the very finest game birds in the world for hunting with trained falcons. They are beautiful, with silvery breast feathers and brown back feathers edged in buff. The deck feathers of the tail are long, and that's what gives them their name. DECK FEATHERS. The middle two feathers in a bird's tail. Their necks, too, are long and elegant, but mostly they are tough. They can withstand unbelievable extremes in weather: fifty below with a wind in winter and a hundred and ten above in summer. They can fly almost like crows, staying up for miles and miles, but they are sprinters, too. In the air they are the size and shape of a two-pound football, twice the size and with five times the resilience of a partridge. Under a falcon they are confident and fly so hard and fast that most stoops are absorbed with little effect. They are the noblest of quarry and their courage is awe-inspiring. Living on the Great Plains, where courage and toughness are so important, it is impossible not to admire them. In fact, for a falconer, sharp-tailed grouse can become an obsession.

We try to keep the grass at an optimum height for sharptail nesting. We plant wheat strips for winter food, keep cattle off the dancing grounds in spring. We've built stock dams in every draw to be sure broods don't go without water. The added perk from this kind of grassland management is a plethora of wildlife. In addition to deer and antelope, there are fox, coyotes, a nest of golden eagles, scores of songbirds, rodents, Hungarian partridge, and lots of ducks. The partridge and ducks are excellent falcon quarry in their own right, so we give them special encouragement.

In fact, the thrust of our management is to make our little ranch a falconer's dream. That everything we do for wildlife is good for cattle is what makes this approach possible. After all, this is the Great Plains, where there are nasty economic realities. There is also the reality of climate. Our country is plagued with hot, dry summers and bitter cold winters. Although the intent is to make our place a paradise, we don't live on a tropical island, and in true Great Plains fashion the dream regularly deteriorates into a nightmare.

The heartbreak of western South Dakota is made greater by the country's mystic power to stimulate optimism. Even people who have lived here their whole lives—and know better—find themselves counting on a chain of events that is completely beyond their control. Unpredictable weather is the big spoiler. Something about this country makes us remember the sixty-degree January days and inclines us to downplay the minus-thirty-degree days. We plan on a nice January and we get our asses handed to us every time.

I have a neighbor with whom I periodically get into some money-making enterprise involving hay or cattle or some other commodity with shaky value. Those schemes often turn out very bad and would never be considered legitimate business deals by anyone but a Great Plains rancher. There is just too much risk in this country. My neighbor is only half-kidding when he says, "I sure hope we break even on this deal. We need the money."

This part of the world has been called "next-year country." Next year prices will be better. Next year it will rain. Next year will be grasshopper-free. Falconry is a "next-year sport." Next year there will be more grouse. Next year the setter will come into his own.

Next year's falcon will be a super bird. Being both a South Dakota rancher and a falconer can be the equivalent of double snakebite. The truth is, things never work out the way you dream them. But maybe it's the wild expectations that make life such a treat. Maybe the payoff is in the dreaming.

By the first of July, Kris and I had already arranged to rent our house in town for a year and the garage and living room were beginning to fill with boxes marked RANCH, NEW HAMPSHIRE, and STORAGE. Kris was madly trying to tie up loose ends so she could leave by July tenth and be ready to start work in Hanover the next week. I had agreed at least to help her drive out, but was still wrestling with my decision on where to spend the autumn. There was the additional consideration that Kris was taking a huge pay cut; it would be extremely helpful if I would hunker down over the word processor and make some money. Hanover, New Hampshire, where I knew almost no one, would be a distraction-free place to do just that.

Erney and I moved the yearlings from one pasture to the next just after lunch, a job that is required every few days. I should have gone back to my desk and worked a few more hours before I quit for the day, but the pending decision had been eating at me for days. Since Kris had been on call the night before and was likely to be at home packing, I thought it would be a good time for a heart-to-heart. I knew Pete Jenny would be calling, wanting to know if I planned to go ahead with the hack, and I needed to have an answer for him. As I drove out of the driveway I looked hard at the hackbox built on the top of the weathering yard. Erney had checked it out; it was ready.

I never know what to expect when I get home to Rapid City from the ranch. Sometimes Kris is there, sometimes she is not, and I always find myself holding my breath as I turn the corner, hoping to see her car in the garage. That day I was in luck. Her Explorer looked like it had crashed into a storage shed. Labeled boxes were piled on all sides; furniture balanced precariously on rolled rugs; brooms, shovels, and rakes sprawled like pickup sticks. I squeezed my truck in as best I could.

Predictably, Kris was in the kitchen. This is her domain and she has more arcane equipment than a French executioner. She knelt on the floor among Calphalon pots, garlic presses, Bundt pans, coffee grinders, canisters, and cutlery. She was wrapping stemware in newspaper and looked up like a puppy loose in the pigeon loft.

The thing I love most about Kris may be her delight in simple things. Her smile is magic, and when she turned it on me that day I felt sure that I couldn't let us be separated any longer than was absolutely necessary. "What are you doing here?" she asked. She wanted to go on, but I stopped her.

"Look, I've been thinking about this fall." I put my back against the refrigerator and slid down to her level.

"Pete Jenny called," she said. "He says the peregrines are ready. He wanted to know what he should do."

"That's what I want to talk about," I said. "I'm not sure it's a good idea for me to stay out here."

"I thought you'd be at the ranch for a few more hours."

"I would have been, but I wanted to talk to you."

"But I told Pete you'd be there. I told him just to bring them over, and give you a call."

"Them?"

"The falcons. He's flying them over right now."

We sat on the floor looking at each other. Then Kris smiled again. "You know you want to do it," she said. "Now hurry up. You'd better get to the airport before Pete." I didn't move. "You want to get them in the hackbox as quick as possible, don't you?"

I nodded my head. The decision had been made. "Come with me," I said.

She looked around the kitchen. It was almost as big a mess as the shop at the ranch. But she couldn't resist a box full of falcon chicks. "Love to," she said.

Pete was just turning onto his landing leg when we pulled up to the Spearfish Airport F.B.O. He flies a classic, old, bright blue Stinson that his kids call Starship Mike. We watched him sideslipping against a crosswind while he waited for the plane to stop flying. The attendant from the F.B.O. came out and stood admiring the plane as Pete taxied to a stop in front of the fuel pump.

Pete Jenny is a long-time friend. He came to work for the Peregrine Fund just about the time I quit the organization to write full time. Now he's a vice president of the Peregrine Fund, Inc. and concentrates his efforts in Central and South America. He's a guy with eclectic interests and an enormous sense of wonder about all kinds of wild things. He and his wife first met Kris on the Yucatán peninsula. While I drank daiquiris and sunned myself by the pool, the three of them spent the afternoon in the jungle behind the hotel catching iguanas. When they dangled their prize catch—about a six-pounder—over my lounge chair, I squealed like a schoolgirl.

In a matter of seconds, Pete and Kris had the box of birds out of the plane and were peeking inside. The three birds were just babies, thirty days old, with flight feathers only three-quarters grown. They were a little young to put into a hackbox, but since ours was so accessible, we could easily give them special care. Each had a head covered with bushy white down. This was the first day they had seen humans up close, and although it was only through a small hole in the top of the cardboard box, they didn't like what they saw. They stared with trepidation at any movement and one of the females hissed like an enraged rattlesnake. That was just the way we wanted them. The idea was to keep them as wild as possible until they were flying strongly, then tame and train them in a three-week blitz.

Pete had raised two of the birds from a pair he had had for years. The mother of the third bird had once belonged to me. Her name was Dolly, and Spud and I had traveled from Montana to the Gulf of Mexico with her one magic autumn ten years ago. The intention of the trip had been to set her free, but that hadn't worked out.

EYAS. A falcon or hawk in its first few months of life; a falcon whose training began as a chick.

Now Dolly was a mother and I was excited to see her offspring and eager to watch her fly. Pete was proud of the eyases. But his boyish smile faded when I pointed out thunderheads building over the Black Hills. He wouldn't get a chance to see the birds put into the hackbox. He'd have to scurry for home.

By then, the Stinson was refueled. We made plans for him to come over and pick up a bird in a month or so. It was, of course, understood that that day might never come. We were both veterans of hacking falcons and knew there were many things that could go wrong. But we didn't dwell on the negatives. We shook hands and Kris and Pete embraced. He wished her luck in New Hampshire and she told him to be careful flying home. Then we watched as the old airplane taxied out for takeoff, turned into the freshening wind from the building thunderstorm, roared its engine, and popped into the air like a child's kite.

In fifteen minutes we were at the ranch and Erney limped out to meet us. He was excited, too. "Ooooh," he said as he peeked in. "Nice flock of chicken hawks."

The sun was starting to slide behind the thunderheads. The evening promised to be a spectacular one and I hoped I could talk Kris into spending the night. But first we had to get the birds into the hackbox.

The weathering yard is where the falcons spend most of their time when we are flying them. It's a wire enclosure twenty-four feet by sixteen feet by eight feet, with a solid back wall to protect the falcons from our northwesterly winds. The other walls and the roof are made of heavy wire mesh, not to keep the falcons in—they are secured to perches with leather leashes—but to keep wild predators out. The rafters that hold the roof wire are built of pressure-treated two-by-eights. They are easily strong enough to hold the three- by four- by three-foot-high plywood hackbox. The box is bolted on top of the weathering yard and faces out to the ranch yard and the dog kennel. There is a ladder attached to the backside of the weathering yard so when the birds are in the box we can easily climb up to feed them without being seen.

Gently extracting falcons from a cardboard box takes some practice. You don't want to get bit or footed, but that's not your main concern. The important thing is to be sure that the falcons are not hurt by you or by their nest mates. The first rule is no fast movements. I never wear gloves. They make it hard to feel what you're doing and they are somehow demeaning to falcons—these are not your garden-variety varmint. If you get footed you can't jerk away. To do so might injure a foot or pull out a talon. Anyway, the chicks are too small to eat you. You have to just hang in there and remember that they're scared to death. They're sure that you're the one who plans to do the eating. Move your hands slowly and if a falcon starts focusing on the hands, move your head gently, with eyes averted, to distract it from what is really happening. Fold the precious wings into the bird's body and hold the falcon firmly. Ease it out as if it were a vial of nitroglycerin. It is possible to mesmerize a bird with gentle movements, and often you can empty a whole box of birds and never cause any fuss.

FOOT. To strike or grab with a foot. Some falcons and hawks are much better than others with their feet.

Other times there is a bloodletting. No matter what happens, though, you have to be sure that none of the blood is the birds'. Sometimes a nasty female explodes and does an acceptable imitation of a Cuisinart. If she does, the main thing is to protect the other birds. That is why, when I saw the look in the eyes of one of the falcons, I stayed away from her until the other two birds had been lifted out, color banded, and placed in the hackbox. Erney was hanging on the ladder, holding the box for me, and had also seen the look in the last falcon's eyes. He smiled when I started in for her. "There's our grouse hawk, Dan'l."

"It takes a hell of a hawk," I said as I slipped my hands lower, "to kill grouse in her first year." And as if the falcon had understood me and took what I'd said personally, she reached out with both feet and footed my hands a dozen times in a split second. She ended with all four talons of both feet sunk into the meat of my hands and her beak locked deep in my thumb. But I had her wings secure against her body and drew her from the box.

Erney smiled as he slipped the red band around her right leg. "She's a dandy," he said.

"Yeah," I squeaked, "a real sweetheart."

By the time all three birds were in the hackbox, the sunset had come on strong. There are only two meteorological features that can be counted on in western South Dakota. One is strong wind and the other is spectacular sunsets. Kris and I sat on the deck with binoculars. We watched the falcons, forty yards away behind the protective bars of the hackbox, as they explored the inside of their new home. Occasionally we leaned back on the picnic table to see how the sunset had changed since we last checked. I had convinced Kris that she should spend the night. It would mean she'd have to get up at four-thirty to make it to work on time but that was all right. We go to bed early at the ranch. Once the sun is down there are only three things to do: eat, read, or indulge in our one admitted creature comfort: sitting in the hot tub and watching the sky.

There wouldn't be much reading that night because we both knew that was probably the last night we'd spend together at the ranch for a long time. We didn't want to waste it on an activity we couldn't share. There was a succulent buffalo roast sizzling in the Weber, fresh corn on the cob ready to boil, and a salad waiting in the refrigerator. Spud lay watching the sunset with us and let out a perfunctory growl every time Mel and Moose made a lap around the house. Eventually Mel gave up the chase and lay down too. But Moose, a springer puppy, continued to make laps at high speed. She charged up one set of steps, thundered across the deck and flew off the other side. She never touched the steps that led down to the hot tub, but spreading her ears, she catapulted herself twenty feet into the yard. She carried a ratty old slipper and couldn't seem to understand why the setters weren't dying to try to take it away.

The evening was warm and we ate the buttered corn and rare buffalo under an enormous sky with star-holes burning brighter as the sun faded in the west. There was a bottle of Merlot and it was more than half gone when we eased into the steaming hot tub.

The older dogs were curled on their beds in the living room under Erney's shelf of orchids and Moose busied herself collecting all the dog toys into one, easy-to-guard pile. The last trace of daylight was gone from the sky. Now the stars were intense and when we rested our heads back on the edge of the tub and stared at them, they seemed to pulse. There wasn't much to say, so we didn't try. We didn't talk about the birds in the hackbox or Kris's faraway fellowship. We let the hot water lull us toward sleep. After a half hour of soaking, Kris's overdeveloped sense of responsibility took control. It was nearly nine-thirty and she had to be sharp the next morning.

We went into the house and I scraped a few dishes while she got ready for bed. Spud and Mel stirred and migrated up the stairs like sleepwalkers and Moose bounced behind dragging a mangled boot. When I went up to the bedroom I found all four of them on the bed, tangled into a pack pile. Only Moose was still awake, and even she was chewing slowly. There wasn't much room for me and I didn't have the heart to evict the dogs just yet.

When I stepped back outside, the moon was coming up huge over the ridge to the east. It cast a whiteness on the prairie that drove the stars back into obscurity. The air was absolutely still and the gravel of the driveway crunched under my bare feet as I made my way to the ladder behind the weathering yard. I eased up the ladder and put my eye to one of the peepholes drilled in the back of the hackbox.

The bars on the front of the box divided the moonlight into vertical strips. The gravel on the floor was white and the shadows of the three sleeping falcons were projected against the side wall. They had had a big day and stood in a line with their heads tucked behind their wings. I was struck by how calmly they seemed to be taking things. But what else could they do? They had no idea what lay ahead.

I turned away from the peephole and sat on the top of the ladder looking at the moon. I wondered what made me think I knew what was in store for them. What made me think I knew what was in store for me? I had a dream of what I thought might happen in the next four months. I hoped all the falcons would fly high and stoop hard, that none of them would fall prey to any of the dangers of the wild. I saw the dogs running hard, finding lots of birds, and making few mistakes. I saw me choreographing it all, shaping events to turn out perfectly.

But I knew no more about the future than did the three falcons sleeping with their heads behind their wings. Because I am human, I knew there were pitfalls ahead, but I could only guess at what they were. I climbed down from the ladder and resolved to give it my best effort. I would have to be careful, demanding, and always firm. I'd start by kicking the dogs out of my bed.

Dog Days

*Y*ou have to wonder what goes through a dog's mind. There are those who say, Not much, but I'm not one of them. When I was a boy it was popular to believe that animals were incapable of thought. Of course, that idea has its origins in some nonsensical, anthropocentric, Christian notion about the hierarchy of animals. Anyone who has seen a pointing dog lock up on a skittish pheasant, glance impatiently over his shoulder as the shooter hurries to get into position, then take off in a sixty-yard arch that puts him in a position where it is impossible to smell the bird might question the dog's intelligence. But you've got to be as smart as the dog. What he's done is put the running bird between himself and the hunter. He's pinned the bird so the shooter will get his shot and he's proved that he can reason—perhaps better than any who might doubt his intelligence.

A veterinarian at the University of Iowa once told me and some friends that the old saying "Dog is a man's best friend" is more than a cliché. This was late at night and there had been many beers in the preceding hours but the old doctor held forth with a professorial gravity that made me believe. "There's a special connection," he said. "They have a much stronger bond to humans than any other species, stronger than horses, or cats, or even falcons." He held a hooded falcon on his fist as he spoke. He was a big man with a beard, a booming voice, and bifocals. He swayed in the firelight with his two golden retrievers looking up at him like they were afraid he might fall. He projected his voice to the assembled group of young falconers. "After all," he said, "they are the only animal to have volunteered for domestication."

The inspired veterinarian claimed dogs were never caught and tamed like other domestic animals but that they followed the camps of early man, drawing closer and closer, until finally the two species were joined in an unprecedented interspecific alliance that has lasted ever since. His speech exhausted him and he sat down between the retrievers and fell silent. The dogs put their heads in his lap and thumped their tails on the floor in canine applause.

The combination of dogs and alcohol prompted another memorable late-night soliloquy years later on the plains of South Dakota. It was a New Year's Eve in the late seventies and I was camped in the snow with Bill Heinrich and Dan Konkel, two old falconer friends from Colorado. The wind had been blowing thirty-five miles an hour all day. It is rightly considered very bad form to drink alcohol while actually flying a falcon. But our birds had been grounded and it was New Year's Eve. We fried up the two pheasants we had caught earlier in the week and ate them along with the pinto beans that had been simmering with a ham bone for three days on the wood-burning stove. We had a big wall tent, but with three people and four dogs it was a little close. We started to bring in the New Year as soon as the sun set. In South Dakota, on the last day of December, that's about four o'clock in the afternoon.

By midnight we were ready to hear each other's New Year's resolutions. We sat on our cots with our dogs curled as close to the stove as they could get without getting off the cots. I can't remember what Bill or I promised to do in the coming year but Dan's resolution is forever embedded in my memory. He's a big, blond, wild ex-wrestler who is known for his low tolerance for alcohol. He had two dogs on that trip: an old, glassy-eyed setter bitch named Jessie and a pup named Lark. He loved these dogs with a passion that was hard to believe of a guy with such rough edges. Both dogs were draped over him and he stroked them as gently as his big hands allowed. When it came his turn to make his New Year's resolution, he didn't look up at us until he had thought it through. His eyes were a bit blurry but his hands never stopped stroking the dogs. He spoke earnestly and twice his voice threatened to break. "This next year," he said, "I want to live my life more like a dog."

We stared at him dumbly. "No, really," he said. "Look at them." He gestured to the dogs in his lap. "Not a phony bone in their bodies. They always have a positive attitude. They live for what's real. Huntin', eatin', fuckin', and fightin'." Dan paused. "But they're loyal. These dogs would do anything for me."

Dan made perfect sense to us that night and I still find truth in what he said. It was certainly true that his old dog, Jessie, was loyal. An hour after we let the Coleman lantern die out, Bill and I heard Dan having trouble keeping his dinner down. The wind was howling and Dan was too incapacitated to leave his bunk. We heard the pheasant and beans splattering on the tent floor. Bill and I wanted no part of this. We pretended to be asleep. There was a heavy silence in the tent as Dan's foggy brain tried to sort out what to do.

Finally we heard his whisper, "Jessie. Here, Jessie. Jessie. That a girl. Good girl." Any doubts we might have had about dogs' desire to do anything for their masters were dispelled when we heard Jessie's reluctant lapping.

My first bird dog's name was Lucky. He had another name when, without parental permission, I brought him, his doghouse, chain, and sack of dog food home. He worked on a hunting preserve and I figured I'd gotten a lot of bird experience for twenty-five bucks. He was a seven-year-old German shorthair. My dad pretended to be outraged by my stupidity; there was obviously something wrong with a twenty-five-dollar dog. That was when Dad started calling the dog Lucky. He figured the preserve owner had bilked me out of twenty-five dollars and saved himself the price of a bullet. Secretly, I think he was pretty proud that his thirteen-year-old son wanted a bird dog bad enough to make such a pitiful deal. I think he also hoped to shoot a few pheasants over old Lucky.

My dad was a dog nut and we had always had dogs. Even though we were pheasant hunters, we'd never had a bird dog and I watched my dad studying Lucky. He was intrigued by this tough old veteran of six seasons of hard pheasant hunting. The dog was big and solid and by July I had him minding as well as any dog my dad had ever seen. But there had to be something wrong with this dog, and it was just a matter of time until it showed itself.

Dad told me the dog probably wouldn't point, that he'd go crazy as soon as he smelled his first bird and that would be the end of it. But when I planted a pigeon for him like I'd seen dog trainers do, Lucky slammed to a stop and stood there while I scared the bird up. He watched it intently as it flew away; he didn't offer to chase it. "Can't be," my dad said. "Got to be something."

I have two brothers and every year, the night before the first day of the hunting season (which was an excused absence from school in those days), we would ceremonially sleep on two sofa beds in a guest bedroom with all the windows open. Since it was the middle of November the nights were often cold, but that was part of the tradition. To this day, I associate the feel of cold air against my face as I sleep with the excitement of the night before the season opener. The night before we tried Lucky out was even more exciting than usual. He was my dog and I knew from the beginning that having your own dog made an already fantastic experience unfathomably better.

Early in the morning our dad came into the room. "Rise and shine. Hit the deck. Jesus Christ, it's colder than Billy Hell in here." We loved it when my dad swore. It was strictly forbidden by our mother, so when he did it we felt somehow closer to him. The idea of being grown up someday didn't seem quite so impossible. We piled out of bed and into our hunting clothes, which meant our old clothes. We were downstairs in the kitchen in time to see Dad bring the first batch of burned pancakes out of the oven.

Only on rare occasions was Dad not at work by the time we got up, and on those mornings my mother stood aside. Only one pheasant opener morning do I remember my mother cooking our breakfast. That year, my dad had to work and, since it was unthinkable that we kids wouldn't go hunting, she took over. It's not that unusual now but in the fifties there weren't many women in the field. Now, every time I see Kris dressed for the hunt I think of my mother, a lady with dungarees tucked into rubber boots and wearing a sweatshirt from my father's college days. She didn't know that much about guns and almost nothing about hunting—she was there to be sure her three boys were safe. She was beautiful.

My mother is renowned for her wisdom, so there probably were several reasons why, on opening day, she would leave the kitchen entirely to us. I wonder if the main reason wasn't the pain of watching my dad cook. She was a bit of a gourmet for those days and there was always plenty of wonderful food around when we were kids. But sauces and soufflés can't hold a candle to breakfasts cooked by your father on the first day of the pheasant season.

To say the least, those meals were unusual. They consisted of stuff we wouldn't have eaten in a million years if our mother had fixed it. There were runny eggs and burnt French toast, hot Italian sausage, lumpy oatmeal, cornmeal mush, and—if Dad had done the shopping—buttermilk and headcheese. I cringe to think of it now, though at the time we loved it, gobbling everything put in front of us. Our favorite was the greasy fried potatoes. I still use Dad's recipe. He started with one yellow onion fried in the grease left from a pound of bacon. In those days all potatoes were peeled before they were cooked but my dad had a certain pioneering flair. Every season opener he committed an act of unheard-of culinary daring by throwing sliced, unpeeled potatoes into the sizzling grease. Just before they were done, he sliced a second onion into the whole mess. We used lots of ketchup and ate every bite.

The rules of engagement were designed for safety. They were simple: only two guns, one shell for each, my older brother got to carry the 12-gauge, my younger brother and I traded off the 20-gauge, Dad was the full-time field marshal. No one knew where Lucky would fit into the scheme, but it was hoped he knew something about hunting and would, at least, kick a few birds into the air. Till that point Lucky had been an easygoing old dog. He slept a lot and didn't get excited about much. But that morning, sitting between me and my younger brother in the backseat of the station wagon, his personality changed. He watched attentively out the windshield. He trembled and whined. He refused to be calmed by ear scratching. My dad glanced at him in the rearview mirror and raised his eyebrows.

It took a few minutes for us to get organized, and Lucky barked from the backseat the whole time. But once the skirmish line was formed and we began to advance through the weedy corn stubble, Lucky started to quarter like a pro. We hadn't gone a hundred yards into the field when his gait went soft. He turned into the wind and pussyfooted to a solid point. After an instant of disbelief, my dad took over. "Scott, move up on the right. Be ready. Mike, leave the gun on safety, move to your left. No, no. Left. That way." He pointed out the exact spot for my little brother. "Handle your dog, Dan. Everybody be careful. I'll flush."

Nobody really believed there was a bird in front of Lucky, so when the rooster pounded from under a crumpled cornstalk there were four exclamations of surprise preceding two completely wild shots. The pheasant sailed, unscathed, across the cornfield. Lucky followed him for thirty feet, then stopped. We all watched the pheasant disappear into a distant grove. "I'll be dipped in shit," Dad whispered.

It took a few minutes to rally the troops. Some strategic changes were made: Scott was given two shells for the 12-gauge pump, Mike was demoted to dog handler, and I was given the old side-by-side 20 and two shells. "All right," Dad said, "let's bear down." He turned to Lucky. "Find the birds, boy."

A hundred yards farther on Lucky slammed onto point and we fanned out into position. The bird came up perfectly. A shotgun roared once—twice. The rooster lined out. A third shot. A fourth. And we all watched the bird follow his buddy into the trees. "Well, for Christ's sake," Dad said.

Then there was silence. We all looked up at him and his gaze moved slowly from face to face. When he finally spoke again his voice was flat and determined. "Give me a gun," he said.

The next two points were hens and Dad held up on them expertly. Scott, Mike, Lucky, and I watched them go and prayed the next would be a rooster. Dad shot left-handed and we figured he was about the best shot in the world. Only now do I understand the pressure that was on the man, and only now do I appreciate his coolness when a rooster did come up. I can see it in slow motion: Lucky pointing again, Scott moving in to flush, the cackle, and the elegant shape catapulting skyward. The gun came up easily, following behind the bird as it leveled off. Dad swung through just as the stock touched his cheek, and the rooster crumpled. I don't remember hearing the shot, but I can still hear the cheers.

The crowd went wild. It was the most fantastic shot ever made and my dad hammed it up, finally raising his hands in a show of false modesty and to ask for calm. When we settled down, Dad sent us out to pick up the pheasant. It had clearly fallen dead and no one thought there would be any trouble finding it. "Right there," Dad said. He pointed and walked right to the spot. But all he found were a few feathers.

"Hey," Mike said. "Where's Lucky?"

We all looked around. No bird and no dog. Then I saw Lucky, running toward us from the far side of the field. He bounced with happiness and came right to my feet for a pet. He didn't look sheepish but his muzzle was covered with dirt.

"The rotten cur," Dad said. "He buried my pheasant." Silence settled on us. We looked at Lucky, who panted and wagged his stubby tail. His front paws carried evidence, too. Everyone stared at him, and he realized that we had found the fault that had made him a liability at the shooting preserve.

We never found that first pheasant. But we ended up taking three birds home that afternoon. It just took a little creative hunting. We divided our efforts into three basic jobs, two shooters, one flusher, and one dog tackler. If the shooters did their job, then the tackler had to do his. And tackling a determined German shorthair in the open field is no easy task. But we got good at it, and even though breaking up the hunting day with wind sprints was frustrating, we came to love that old dog. He certainly made bird hunting more interesting and helped set the course of my life. I haven't ventured into the field without a dog since.

Since the days of Lucky there have been many dogs. Though it has been a while since I've had a dog with a vice as severe as bird burying, I've never had a perfect one either. The one thing you can say with certainty about dogs is that every one is different. The summer Kris was getting ready to head east we had three dogs that proved that point.

Idaho Spud was ten years old that summer. He's a black and white English setter from a big running strain in the Northwest. To date, he's the best bird dog I've ever had and has gained some fame in falconry circles for his brains and his ability to find birds. A few people have thought enough of him to have him sire litters, and that spring he had hosted a nice little bitch from Wyoming for a romantic weekend. Since then he had been feeling pretty frisky, but he was no pup and there was a hitch in his gait that bothered me.

He had never been a dog to take care of himself. He's a sweetheart, always ready for a pet or a cuddle, but he's tough as rawhide. He'll run in ice and snow, sandburs, swamps, through barbed wire and broken glass. He's been lost overnight in below-zero weather, been stomped by cows, fallen off cliffs, killed coons, cats, badgers, and one coyote. He's pointed every North American game bird, including wild turkeys. In ten seasons I'd never seen him quit or even slow down. So even though he might have earned that little hitch in his gait, it surprised me. I guess I never thought he'd grow old.

Taking a closer look, I saw that his hindquarters were no longer like Christmas hams, his muzzle had grayed, his coat had lost some sheen, and there was an incipient clouding in his eyes. I still thought of him as the hard-headed puppy he had been until his third year. He had been a nightmare to break, a happy, playful dog, with a fantastic way of going, but a bird-chasing maniac. Even at ten, you had to talk tough to him if you wanted him to hold his birds. But boy, could he find them. When it soaked in that Spud might not be around forever, I took a good look at his backup.

WAY OF GOING. The quality of a dog's gait; the way he carries himself.

Old Hemlock Melville is a big, goofy, slow-moving setter from one of the most famous lines in the world. He was just coming on four that summer but in many ways was still a puppy. Even though his lack of speed made him something of a mismatch for our big rolling grasslands, he had won a solid place in our hearts.

HONOR. The action of a dog when it freezes upon seeing another dog on point. Usually only the first dog scents the birds.

Mel thinks that Spud is the greatest dog on earth, his hero, and he will honor Spud's points from any distance. I had high hopes for Mel as a falcon dog; so far, however, he was finding only half as many birds as Spud. Though he had only a fraction of Spud's drive, he was a gentleman, a

BACK. The action of a dog when it stops behind another dog that is on point. Generally, both dogs can scent the game.

natural backer who made few mistakes. While Spud found lots of birds, he mishandled many of them. Mel didn't find as many but he was careful, smart, and, above all, hunted with you. Because Mel looked at hunting as a team sport, he was a piece of cake to handle.

From his first year on, he was Kris's buddy and favorite hunting partner.

On our annual woodcock hunt in New Brunswick the fall before, Mel had come on strong. Again, he hadn't found the birds that some of the other dogs had; when he found one, though, he found it within sight of the hunters and held it. His long feathering, massive head, sad eyes, and old-fashioned low tail can't help but make you feel like part of an oil painting as you walk in front of him with your double-barrel held high. When you hunt with Mel, there are no extended expeditions deep into unknown woodcock swamps in search of the distant signal from a beeper collar. No yelling is necessary, no discipline. He's a pleasure to hunt with even if you aren't shooting birds. He moves at his slow pace and saves himself for the cocktail party afterward. The classic Old Hemlock head and shiny orange belton coat look great in front of the fire at the lodge. If we'd allow it, Mel would drink single-malt Scotch and smoke a pipe. He's an amiable dog who enjoys the company of other hunters. He seems to have trouble understanding why the rest of the dogs are too exhausted to join the party.

BELTON. A color phase of dog, usually an English setter, in which the black or orange is distributed in very small spots over a coat of white.

COVER. An area that is likely to hold birds, usually woodcock or ruffed grouse. Sometimes called covert.

Mel's saggy face surprises some people. To those used to modern setters he might look more like a thin Saint Bernard, but he is a gun hunter's dream, especially if the hunting is done in the close cover he was bred for. Sharp-tailed grouse live in five-thousand-acre fields with no trees in sight, however, and Mel had not proved himself in that terrain. At his New Brunswick pace it would take Mel a month to hunt five thousand acres. His brains and biddability might make the difference, yet when I looked at him in light of Spud's advanced years, I got nervous. If Spud pooped out on me and Mel wasn't yet ready to come off the bench, what would I do?

There was one other possibility. For the past four years our woodcock hunt had included a guide who specialized in close-working springer spaniels. His springers are small and attentive and can be tucked away, by the half dozen, in a setter-size dog box. Though they're energetic and happy, they're short-legged and dumpy compared to the tall, feathered setters around which the hunt revolves. They look like dwarf setters with bobbed tails, the kind of dog Danny DeVito might own. They snort and wiggle in an ignoble way and have been tagged with the affectionate nickname of the trolls. The banter between the springer and the setter folks goes on the entire week. While it's agreed that setters bring a certain quality to the hunt, it is also the overwhelming opinion of both sides that the springers are more efficient for bringing birds to the bag. They're little machines; it's like turning a pack of Hoover vacuums loose in a cover. Whatever's in the bushes comes out, and it comes out within shotgun range. If it gets shot, it gets retrieved. You don't lose birds when there is a troll along. And you never lose a troll, either. In fact, they're forever underfoot wanting to know what you want them to do next. Over the years I came to love these little monsters and thought they might have a tremendous application in the kind of falconry we do on the Great Plains. The British use similar dogs to flush ptarmigan that have been pointed by other dogs, something I'd always thought made sense. I've encouraged some of my setters to flush, and that, of course, softens their points. But if you flush yourself, the quarry makes the decision when to go. Whether you're forty feet or two inches away, a grouse will wait until the falcon is in less-than-perfect position. We also fly at a lot of grouse and partridge that are not pointed—a flock settles into a grainfield ahead of us, a few heads are spotted in the grass. I thought situations like this cried out for a troll, so when I heard that our guide had a new litter, I told him to pick a small, smart, active bitch and send her down.

We named her Moose, not for her size but in honor of her home province of New Brunswick. The name is versatile and can serve as a nickname for *mus musculus* (the scientific name for house mouse), or the more feminine Moose-Anne. She is exactly what I ordered: small, smart, and unbelievably active. She never stops moving. From the day she arrived she's been flying around the house and yard, her front feet hitting the ground with half the frequency of her hind feet. There is always something in her mouth—her coveted slipper, a ball, a stick, a chunk of firewood, a deer bone, a stone, a dead mouse, a horse apple, a screwdriver. She must have slept in the first six months we had her but I never caught her at it. By the time Mel has gathered himself to jump into the back of the pickup, Moose has sailed up and down a half-dozen times. She is a 45 RPM dog in a 33⅓ world. I had no idea what might happen if I had to elevate her to a starting position on the grouse team.

FALCON. Purists follow the ancients' lead and use the term falcon to refer only to the female peregrine falcon. But it also can mean a female of any species of falcon. A still more general usage applies to any of the long-winged birds of prey, male or female, as opposed to the short-winged hawks.

A sobering thought was that all my worry about having a good dog to use on sharptails that fall might well be moot. The falcon I hoped to get back from the hack was no sure thing. First, the chances of losing her at hack were great, and second, few first-year birds are really good grouse hawks. I figured I'd be lucky to catch a dozen partridge with her. That left me with the old intermewed falcons.

Little Bird was a fourth-year Barbary falcon that we had flown almost exclusively at release Hungarian partridge. She was a beautiful bird with a light slate back and a buff front with a few delicate horizontal flecks of black. Her manners were perfect, and she was easy to hood and pick up off a kill or the lure, and tame as a house cat, if she liked you. If she didn't, though, or if you wore a hat or were a dog she'd never seen before, she lost her mind. Erney had a special relationship with Little Bird; I was just tolerated.

She flew at just under twenty ounces, and could put on a show. When she was on her game, she flew as well as any bird I've ever seen. Her normal pitch was in the realm of "just a speck," and from that height partridge had no chance—unless, of course, she decided not to drive through them the way the really good ones always do. When Little Bird was cast off, you could be sure she'd go up high and wait on, but that was about it. In the three years we'd flown her she'd caught a lot of release partridge, many of them in great style, but she'd never looked at a duck and she'd bounced off grouse like a tennis ball. She had gained a reputation as a temperamental sandbagger. I didn't have a lot of hope for making her a first-rate game hawk, but my plan was to try.

Dundee was a second-year, fully hacked Australian peregrine tiercel with an unusually sweet disposition. We flew him at about eighteen ounces, but weight didn't seem to matter. He was the kind of bird that was always happy to see you. He would bate at you even with a full

LURE. The usually leather pouch garnished with meat and swung to call a falcon to the falconer. Falcons are fed on the lure.

CAST. A pair of falcons flown together. Also, to hold a falcon or hawk, as when jesses and bells are being attached. Also, to launch a bird into the air from the fist; to cast off.

WAIT ON. To go to a height above the falconer and dogs and stay there until the game is flushed.

GAME HAWK. This term does not usually refer to hawks at all but to a falcon trained to catch game birds from a pitch.

BATE. To fly from the fist or a perch and be brought up short by the leash. This is to be avoided.

crop and would crawl onto your fist when you were tying another bird to the perch beside him. When you raised the hood to him, he would stand on tiptoe to get his head inside and anyone could handle him. But those endearing characteristics don't make a good game hawk and, in fact, he was a lousy hawk: the only bird I know of that never did learn to wait on.

CROP. The membranous pouch in the gullet of a bird where food is stored before it is digested.

His poor showing as a game hawk was, no doubt, my doing. I had made him a mar-hawk. For decades, I have harbored a desire to fly falcons "out of the hood" instead of the more traditional, "waiting on" style of flying. When a falcon waits on she is allowed to gain altitude over the quarry before it is flushed. When a falcon is flown out of the hood, the quarry is flushed when the falcon is still hooded and on the fist. At the flush, the hood is struck and the chase begins. It is admittedly a more basic approach, but natural, and very demanding. It's the kind of falconry practiced in Arab countries, but because we in North America are so heavily influenced by British falconry, we look down on flying out of the hood, even though much of our terrain and quarry are perhaps better suited to that style.

MAR-HAWK. A bird that has been spoiled in some way by the falconer.

I did it seriously one year when the grouse population around the ranch crashed and the white-tailed jackrabbit population skyrocketed. I had great fun that winter with a gyrfalcon, a sharp-shod cow horse we used to rope calves in the spring, and a muzzled Saluki given to me by a Canadian falconer friend. Galloping over the treacherously icy prairie in pursuit of falcon, dog, and ten-pound rabbit whetted my appetite for that kind of falconry. (It also, incidentally, confirmed something I always suspected but didn't want to admit: that things are even more interesting if there's a chance you'll get killed.)

I thought flying a falcon out of the hood would be easy compared with training it to wait on. And it might be, if you know what you're doing. But I didn't and Dundee suffered for my ignorance. Even though he had spent thirty days flying at hack, he never really caught on to flying birds down. By the time I decided to give up, it was too late to get him back on track for waiting on.

Erney and I agreed that we had ruined him. Because he'd had a lot of air time, was in great physical shape, and had had his hack, we tried to turn him loose the spring of his first year. He wouldn't go. He hung around and picked off our homing pigeons using a variety of ignominious methods, until we brought him in and kept him. I think it made everyone happy. Dundee was glad to get back into his mews and Erney and I were glad to have such a cheerful little guy around.

Erney had given up on making him a hunting hawk of any kind for good reasons. Now with this chance to devote full time to falconry, I believed it was possible to get him catching birds. In fact, I thought the stars might be right to get a falcon performing on doves, and that Dundee might be the bird.

But my main hope for a successful season was in the hackbox. The day before I left to drive Kris to New Hampshire, Erney and I sat on the deck planning just how we hoped the hack would go. The three falcons would stay in the box another five days. That would give me time to drive Kris to New Hampshire and the falcons time to mature to the point of being able to fledge. I'd fly back from Boston the evening before we opened the box and let the birds free. All Erney had to do was check on the falcons and feed them, skipping the last day's feeding to ensure that they'd be hungry enough to stick around long enough to at least get the lay of the land before they tried their wings. We'd both be on hand for those critical first days of liberty.

We sat at the picnic table sipping our coffee and trying to think if we had forgotten anything. We stared out to the east and watched as a mule deer doe herded her twins out of the draw and into some distant plum bushes. In the summertime we spend a lot of time on the deck, looking out over the big draw that is continually offering up natural phenomena like the doe and her fawns. We use the deck as an observation platform and I have no idea how we ever got along without it.

Erney and I built it and put a pair of sliding glass doors on the east side of the old house five years before. As with almost all our projects, there was grave debate over construction philosophy. Erney is a minimalist. He believes it's a waste to build anything bigger or stronger than absolutely necessary. I, on the other hand, tend to overbuild. Too often I have seen South Dakota weather twist and smash structures that were underdesigned. Discussion about size of foundations, distance between joists, even number of nails per board, can get heated. But in the end things do get built.

The deck has a great view to the east and south and would give us a clear view of the hackbox if the Russian olive tree at the edge of the deck weren't doing so well. Growing trees on the Great Plains is like growing cactus in Alaska. They're not meant to be there and it takes ingenuity and tenacity to get them to survive, let alone thrive. The reason for the Russian olive's health is that when we built the deck, we ran the downspout from the roof under the deck and into the tree's basin. It gets twenty times the normal rainfall and as a result is the fastest growing tree in the county. We're pretty proud of it but it does make it hard to sit at the picnic table and see exactly what's going on at the hackbox.

As Erney and I sat talking, we periodi- KAKKING. A noise made by excited falcons.
cally glanced through the branches of the Russian olive and sometimes caught the movement of one of the birds behind the protective bars of the box. We weren't paying much attention; there was some movement, a bird was flapping. Then there was kakking and Erney and I shot to our feet. It was the noise used to ward off trespassers. We immediately thought of the golden eagles who were nesting on the east side of the ranch. They could be deadly to falcons, so I jumped to the deck's lower level, intending to reveal myself fully and scare off whatever might be harassing the falcons. There was no eagle, but I caught a small brown flash as it disappeared around the barn.

"What was it?" Erney asked.

I shook my head. I wasn't sure. "Had to be an accipiter of some kind."

ACCIPITER. A genus of raptor with short wings and a long tail, known for short bursts of speed. Accipiters are true hawks, represented in North America by the sharp-shinned hawk, Cooper's hawk, and goshawk.

"Yep," Erney said, as if that was what he expected. "There was a baby Cooper's hawk trying to catch the pigeons yesterday."

"Great," I said. A Cooper's hawk is smaller than a peregrine and probably wouldn't hurt them, but it could cause all sorts of trouble during a hack. "Well, we may have to do something about him," I said, though I didn't know quite what could be done.

Kris and I left the Black Hills on a Tuesday. I had a flight out of Boston on Saturday and the falcons would be released on Sunday. The plan was to drive through Minnesota, across the Upper Peninsula of Michigan, cut across Ontario to Montreal, then travel straight down to Hanover, New Hampshire. The drive was over two thousand miles so there wasn't much extra time, but if Jim Harrison was going to be at his cabin in northern Michigan, we wanted to stop and visit. If it was possible, we wanted to view him in his native habitat.

Jim is a well-known writer, hunter, fisherman, gourmet, and gourmand, connoisseur of all manner of earthly delights. I first met him in a motel in Rapid City, South Dakota. He was passing through with another writer, Dan Gerber, and called to tell me he had read one of my books, *The Rites of Autumn*, and liked it. He wanted to meet me. I'd never heard his gravelly voice and assumed someone was playing a trick on me. All my friends knew he was something of a hero of mine. Kris and I both half-expected a gang of people to jump out of the motel room and have a good laugh on us.

But it really was Harrison. He roared for us to come in. The first thing he did was to offer us a glass of whiskey. "Sorry," he said. "We don't have any mix. There might be some ice, if you want it."

That was a good start and things warmed up from there. The evening culminated at a Chinese restaurant, where Harrison ordered for everyone. "We'll take page two," he said to the waitress. "And don't bring any of those little boxes. We'll eat it here." It was a grand evening. Kris and Jim hit it off and kept up a continuous chatter about food and cooking techniques. We made plans for Jim and Dan to come out to the ranch the next day to watch me work a very young falcon.

Jim is a big guy. He really does remind me of a bear. He's built like a bear and talks like a bear would talk. There is also a genuine wildness to his face due, in part, to a glass eye that is permanently fixed on the horizon. He claims to have lost the eye in grade school, in his first encounter with a woman. Jim's looks belie the man underneath. He is generous, curious, and sensitive to all sorts of animals. With the possible exception of English setters—he is the one who recommended Melville's line to me—birds seem to be his favorite, and he was fascinated by the falcon we flew that morning.

The bird was just a beginner and I was trying to encourage him to go up high and wait on. I had brought one of our homing pigeons to toss out for him as a reward if he did happen to go up even a hundred feet. He was not experienced enough to catch a pigeon, unless it did something stupid, but he loved to chase them.

Jim watched the falcon leave my fist and circle us as we stood in the middle of a thousand-acre flat of wheat stubble and grass. His functional eye followed the flight and a grin came across his face. The falcon was going up and I knew that when I threw the pigeon, Jim's grin would explode into a smile. I flipped the pigeon out and when the falcon started his stoop I turned to watch Jim.

There was this block of a man, a mile from the nearest cover of any kind, with his legs spread and his hands on his hips. Were it not for the glass eye, the look on his face could have been that of a joyous and innocent child. But as I watched him, the smile began to fade. I looked back toward the birds and saw that the pigeon had turned. The falcon was right on its tail and it was heading for the only haven in sight, Harrison.

Jim's face went ashen. The shadow of the plummeting birds came over him and he looked like a heavy, one-eyed Wile E. Coyote about to be leveled by an anvil. But Jim can move a lot faster than you might think. The instant the pigeon took refuge behind his left leg and a split second before the falcon piled in talons first, the big man dived to the right. He landed on his stomach ten feet from where the falcon and pigeon rolled in a feathered tangle. The earth shook and a small puff of dust rose.

I was doubled over with laughter and even Jim had to smile. He rolled into a sitting position and spit out some dirt. "I thought the little son of a bitch was going for my good eye," he said.

When we called Jim, he said our timing was good. He was just heading up to his cabin to get some work done. He added that his wife, Linda, had been after him to lose some weight for the upcoming bird season, and he thought isolation might help. We could meet there, spend the night, and get out early the next morning. That was perfect. It took us most of the day to cross the top of Wisconsin and run almost the entire length of the Upper Peninsula. We passed through hundreds of miles of woodcock and grouse covers and threatened to return some day to check them out. The sun was low over Lake Superior when we took a thirty-second tour of the tiny town closest to Jim's cabin.

Ten minutes later we came to a dirt driveway angling off into the Northwoods. From our written directions, this had to be the place, but there was a big sign telling us to keep out. Maybe this wasn't right. We drove on down the back road but found nothing and returned to the sign. With reservations we began our winding descent into the bush. It looked like a good ruffed grouse cover, just the kind of place I expected, but there were more discouraging signs. KEEP OUT. GO BACK. NO TRESPASSING. But we pushed on and slowly the signs began to take on a certain Dantean ring.

We were on the right track and two twists of the road later we pulled into an idyllic clearing with a trout stream moving in front of a small but substantial log cabin. It had to be the right place. It was like stepping into Jim's book *Sun Dogs*. A Land Cruiser was pulled up beside the house with its back door flung open. What looked like a medium-sized black bear in Bermuda shorts and flip-flops was rooting through boxes and books piled in the back.

Jim turned to give Kris a hug and to shake my hand. "Good to see you. I just got here myself. I was thinking about dinner."

"I thought Linda had you on a bird-hunter's diet," Kris said with a little ribbing in her voice.

"She packed a box of food for me," Jim said, and turned back to the car. Kris and I leaned over his shoulder as he pawed through the box. He checked everything out closely, then let his head drop. "Just as I thought," he said. "A fucking whole-grain nightmare."

Then he reached deeper into the car and brought out another box: "Good thing I stopped on the way and did some shopping." He led the way into the cabin, and in the box he carried I could see at least two bottles of wine resting on a bundle of white butcher's paper.

The cabin's kitchen was functional but small. I, being unskilled labor, was chased out to start the charcoal while Jim built the salad and Kris peeled and crushed garlic. When I came back inside for a second glass of cabernet, Kris and Jim were happily slicing away at twin cutting boards and talking about the virtues of jicama. I looked over Kris's shoulder and saw that she had already crushed a handful of garlic. She took one more head from a brown paper bag, held it up, and asked Jim if he wanted her to do another one. Jim looked at the pile on the cutting board. "Oh," he said, "might as well do them all." He reached over and dumped out the bag. There were at least ten more heads.

When Kris and I looked at him in disbelief, he shrugged. "It's not a seasoning," he said. "It's a vegetable."

The plan was to rub all the garlic into the meat he'd bought. When he pulled the bloody package from the box I couldn't believe my eyes. It looked like a mastodon steak, but Jim assured us it was beef. It had to weigh six pounds and when he rolled it, encrusted with a half-inch glaze of garlic, onto the grill, I worried it would put my fire out.

But it cooked just fine, well done for the outside quarter-inch and cooling to a full inch-and-a-half center strip of cherry red Black Angus. The garlic was perfect, the salad and sugar peas just right. There was plenty of good red wine and we talked about books, politics, and brook trout.

I had done most of the driving that day and so I faded first. I crawled up into the loft and flopped on the bed. The reflection of the fire played on the ceiling and I rolled over to point my good ear to the conversation about the philosophy behind a novel Jim was working on, then about Kris's fellowship. The last thing I remember hearing was a discussion about the ethics of critical-care medicine: When do you pull the plug on a terminally ill patient? The voices sounded wise. The people below, sitting in front of the fire, sounded mature and responsible. They were engaged in the vital organs of life and I couldn't help but wonder if the same could be said of me. Could a passion for grass and falcons be compared with concern for human pain and the philosophies that might explain such suffering? Maybe it was the wine, but stretched out on that bed, knowing what the next four months held for me, I felt trivial, like a stevedore who works the deck but knows nothing of how the ship is run.

There was just enough garlic steak left for a grand breakfast and as I slid into the driver's seat I joked that I'd have to hold my hand over my mouth every time we stopped for gas. Jim was shaking my hand. "If they don't like garlic," he said, "fuck 'em."

After clearing customs at Sault Sainte Marie, we began the long, mostly single-lane trek to Montreal. I have always liked Canada and Canadians. The people have a great attitude about life, like Australians, only coherent. A higher percentage of Canadians hunt than Americans and they drink more beer. They have more wild country than just about any other place on Earth. But parts of the diagonal across Ontario, from the Sault to Montreal, are not pretty.

There was heavy summer traffic, and everything—bridges, roads, gas stations—seemed to be under construction. It took half again as long as it should have, and were it not for the ripe blueberries being sold cheap along the road, it would have been torture.

Mining had made a moonscape around Sudbury, but the bushes that were struggling back were purple with blueberries. To add to the poor traffic conditions, the cars of local pickers were stopped haphazardly at every imaginable turnout. Because we were already behind schedule, we didn't even try to pick our own. We pulled to a halt at a rickety stand and bought the smallest basket for sale. That was two kilos of blueberries, enough to give an entire Boy Scout troop terminal dysentery.

We were careful and Kris meted out the sweet berries as if they were prescription drugs. It was a fine fruit experience. That was all we ate until we crossed back into the United States. There were still several pounds of blueberries in the basket and we had to make a special stop and bury them in the back of the Explorer under the stereo, where we couldn't get at them. We couldn't bring ourselves to throw them away.

Our last night on the road was spent in Burlington, Vermont. The plan was to get into Hanover the next morning, find Kris's rental house, and get things moved in. The next day we'd be off to Boston, and I'd catch a plane to South Dakota.

The house had been billed as a country place where we would be able to keep a couple of dogs when I finally came out to stay. The roads in South Dakota are straight. If you miss someone's place by a mile or two, you are usually in sight of it. You just go to the next road and head back in the right direction. I learned pretty quickly that New England is not like that. It took a while to find the house, but finally the country opened into a five-acre field and there it was, a nice, little yellow house surrounded by ruffed grouse woods and within twenty minutes of Dartmouth-Hitchcock Hospital. When I saw a tree, bigger than anything on the ranch, growing up through the ancient stone wall running in front of the house, the feeling that had been just under the surface throughout the drive came out. I was gripped with regret. Suddenly, I wasn't sure I wanted to leave.

The no-nonsense, New England landlady met us in the driveway. She went through the operation of the house like it was the preflight checklist for a Phantom jet. As I listened to her explanation of how the electric heat worked and when the recycling would be picked up, I thought she would be relieved if she knew what it takes to maintain a place where humanity's grip on the land is still tenuous. The stone wall that separated this pleasant front yard from the cultivated forest beyond was almost two hundred years old when the first white settler laid eyes on the land that is now our ranch. She was worried about her house deteriorating. When I think about taking care of a place, I think in terms of keeping it from disappearing altogether. It didn't look like there was much danger of that happening here, but we listened to all her warnings and feigned close attention to her suggestions.

It was not yet noon when we were left alone. We unloaded most of the car, then went to town for lunch. Ten years before, Kris had been a medical student here and a few of the good restaurants from that era survived. She took me to a charming Italian place on the main street of Hanover and we ate a lunch you simply cannot find in Rapid City, South Dakota.

After the meal we went to a café down the street and sat watching the Dartmouth summer students pass outside the window. The café was called the Dirt Cowboy for reasons I still don't understand. I'd be willing to bet that I was the closest thing to a cowboy that had ever scarfed a scone in that establishment. There were no shitty boots, no sweaty hatbands, no puckered Copenhagen lips.

Everyone who came in the café or passed the front wore frumpy L. L. Bean clothes and pale New England complexions. Sitting at the window table in new Patagonia shorts, enjoying a double latte mocha, I had to smile. It was that luscious feeling of getting away with something, like being mistaken for the groom at a high-society wedding.

It was after dark when we finished settling Kris into the house. The day had been warm and humid and the night didn't cool the way it does in South Dakota. I didn't sleep well. It was impossible for me not to be reminded of Kris's old dog, Jake.

For ten years Kris has carried a photograph of me in her wallet. In the picture, I'm kneeling in front of a reservoir not five miles from where I lay sleepless that night. I'm wearing a heavy coat and looking very young. My arms are wrapped around a big black dog. The dog has a red bandanna around his neck and we are both clearly happy. Kris claims it's her favorite picture.

Kris's affinity for dogs is nearly paranormal. She has a knack for knowing what they're thinking and what they want. But when we first met, her attraction to dogs was indiscriminate, embracing schizophrenic Pomeranians as passionately as it did finely focused English pointers. This, I was sure, was because she had never seen a dog doing what a dog does best—hunting. I like to think that it was my influence that created in Kris an understanding and love for hunting dogs, what they do, and how they can enrich your life. But lying there trying to sleep in that sultry New England night, I understood that the real credit had to go to Jake. He knew her long before I was on the scene.

Kris was raised in Southern California. She never had the chance to see a trained dog locate, point, or retrieve a bird. But she had a good companion when I first met her. Jake was an eighty-pound Lab–golden retriever cross that had been with her since she started medical school. One of the first serious things she ever said to me was that she wouldn't have made it through if it weren't for Jake.

He was with her the whole way, bounced around from city to city, keeping her company when she was studying, and sometimes waiting indoors for sixteen hours at a stretch until she could get home to walk him. She told me that some nights, when she got home, the combination of long hours and sub-zero temperatures conspired to depress her to tears. But Jake was always there to greet her and they walked every night, and that's what gave her the strength to get up the next morning and do it again.

That she had learned the restorative powers of a relationship with a dog told me she was special. And that Jake had been the one to teach her made him special, too. I had always dreamed of finding a woman who would enjoy being afield with me and a dog, and those two gave me hope that that might not be too far-fetched.

Jake got his looks from his Lab side. Except for slightly longer hair, you'd never have known he wasn't pure Lab. He had one of those heads that could have been carved from granite, and a gentle way of looking at you—as if he felt vaguely sorry for you, being human and all. Like so many of the really good ones, Jake seemed to know how he could best support the people with whom he lived. After Kris moved on to her internship and residency, when she had even less time, and I started hanging around more, Jake shifted a portion of his allegiance to me. I'm sure he knew it was what Kris wanted, and I was grateful to be included.

After medical school Kris engineered a two-year residency in Denver, and since it was only three hundred miles away from the ranch, I took to spending a lot of time there. I was used to sleeping alone, and while sharing a bed with Kris was a welcome change, sharing a bed with Kris and Jake was not exactly what I had had in mind. I remember coming face to face with Jake one of those first nights. He stared at me unflinchingly and I realized that it was I who was the interloper here. I was infringing on the unity of a serious, well-functioning team, and so Jake stayed on the bed.

During residency Kris was putting in fourteen-hour days with every third night on call. Jake and I were thrown together and it was good for both of us. Her house was on a busy street. The traffic was confining—something new for me—and Jake and I used it as a good excuse to escape the city.

We began going on extended walks in more remote places than Jake was used to. Kris was a little protective of him, suggesting, for example, that he wouldn't eat dog food without cooking oil on it and that November water was too cold for him to retrieve sticks from. She made it sound as if Jake preferred tofu to T-bones. But after I started taking him to the ranch and he met Spud, who was just a pup then, and an old basset hound named Morgan, I came to know something about Jake that I had suspected all along.

Morgan had been an ace-high rabbit-hawking dog, but was retired by then. He was like an old demented pensioner returning to the office out of habit. He got up early, had a little drink of water, and usually struck a trail about seven-thirty. He'd work that rabbit until about noon, come into the house for another drink, and snooze until about four o'clock, when he'd get drowsily to his feet, stretch, amble to the door, and let out one assertive bellow. He'd run another bunny for the rest of the day. A little while after dark he'd come in to eat and sleep and it would start all over again the next morning. When I think of Morgan I think of James Gavin's description of scent in his book *The Meadow*. He saw it as a vaporous blue contrail that fades with time. I love to imagine being able to see those streaks and watching old Morgan sorting through them to find the brightest one.

He was slow and inefficient but he'd had hundreds of rabbits caught by hawks in front of him. To my knowledge Morgan never caught a rabbit on his own. When he came baying up on the jumble of fur and feather at the end of the trail, he would simply turn and go find another track. I'm not sure he ever even saw a rabbit without a red-tailed hawk stuck to it. He must have thought he was trailing some sort of griffin-type beast, part hawk, part rabbit.

Morgan took his work seriously and didn't pay much attention to this big, black, city dog who stayed in the house. But several times I caught Jake watching Morgan from the kitchen window, studying the old-timer as he snooped through the overgrown haying equipment, and it wasn't long before the black ears came up and the eyes danced at the sound of Morgan's strike.

Jake acted indifferent when he saw me picking up a falcon and heading out to hunt, but he couldn't help glancing at Spud and me as we went through yard training. The whole ranch scene, with its cacophony of bird noises and new smells, made him a little nervous and though he disdained close contact with Spud and Morgan, he couldn't help being interested. When Kris came out to the ranch and made a fuss over these two ruffians, it threw Jake into a tailspin.

It was about that time that Kris began to take an interest herself—in me, I suppose, but more specifically, in the elements of my life. She asked about the falcon hoods, the electric collar, the dog boxes and hawk perches built into the back of the pickup. She watched Spud point a grouse wing and was fascinated by the way this little moron puppy went deadly serious over a game. She watched steady old Morgan going about his appointed rounds and began to see how important it all was to me.

After about the third visit, she wondered if, the next time, she might try shooting a shotgun and I, of course, bent over backward to comply. I planned to let her shoot my side-by-side 20 but Erney shook his head. "That's a mistake," he said. "She won't hit anything and a light little thing like that will kick her silly." When Kris arrived at the ranch for her first shooting lesson, I had a brand-new Remington 1100 12-gauge with open choke and a shortened stock waiting for her—ugly, but no kick and maximum chance for success.

Before there was any shooting, however, we had to put Jake in the basement. Though he'd never seen a gun before, he was apparently shy of explosions. Kris said he spent most of every Fourth of July trying to get under the refrigerator.

I had a hard time believing it. With little Spud pistoning in his kennel and poor old blind Morgan limping out to investigate every dead clay pigeon, it was hard to imagine that a dog like Jake wouldn't want in on the fun. But it was clear he did not.

After shooting practice, Kris and I came into the house full of good thoughts about the possibility of Kris joining me on a pheasant hunt. The season was half over by then but there might be a way to get in some sort of hunting. She was delighted with the shotgun and the shooting. I was delighted that she was delighted. She even mentioned the idea that Jake might go with us on the hunt.

But when we went into the basement, we found Jake quaking in a corner. It was a terrible sight and my ebullience drained when Kris put her arms around Jake and apologized for shooting. I felt the plans for a pheasant hunt and a woman to share my days in the field slipping away. But it was a dream worth fighting for and I vowed right there that I would.

Thank God Jake loved cheese more than he feared anything.

Kris was skeptical, but after Jake figured out that the sound of a cap gun wrapped in a towel meant cheddar, it wasn't long until the towel was discarded. Another week and you didn't want to be between him and the kitchen when the starter's pistol went off. Finally he'd come full bore across any field for a 12-gauge shot—and a quarter-pound of Gouda.

We at least had a chance. Dog over his gun-shyness, new shotgun, first-time hunter—this had the potential to be fun. But there was another catch. On a picnic during a rare medical school break, when Jake was just a puppy, he had wandered off and been caught in a chicken coop, knee-deep in fresh-plucked chickens. It was the first time Jake had ever seen birds up close but the owner of the chickens wasn't in a forgiving mood and whacked him across the nose. "He hasn't shown much interest in birds since," Kris said.

She swore the punishment had been extremely mild—only a crisp thump across the muzzle—and I assured her that there would be no problem. Jake didn't mind gunfire anymore and he loved to retrieve. His natural instincts would take over and he'd do fine. That's what I told her. But I'd gotten to know Jake pretty well by then and knew he learned lessons for keeps. I was worried that his desire to do what people wanted him to do might extend to that New Hampshire chicken farmer. In an attempt to avoid a bad day in the field, I took a Hungarian partridge a falcon had killed the day before to where Jake and I normally played fetch with tennis balls and sticks.

He leaped and twisted with joy when I held the stick over his head and sat, trembling with anticipation, when I gave the command. I threw the stick twice and he pounded after it, delivering it to hand when I asked. The third time I surreptitiously substituted the partridge from my pocket for the stick and sent him off after it with an encouraging "Fetch." He bore down on the partridge like a hungry goshawk, but never laid a tooth on it. As soon as he recognized it as a bird he pulled up like it was a cow pie and trotted quickly back to my side. He looked up at me as if I'd pulled the dirtiest trick in the book. I had a problem.

All I could think was that Kris was counting on a pheasant hunt. I tried to reassure Jake by putting my arm around him. He turned his head from me and I knew I'd better get him back into retrieving quick. I got Jake's favorite toy—a green, day-glo Frisbee—and this snapped him out of his paranoia. He did the happy-dog dance, complete with leaps and yips, and I sailed the Frisbee out for him to chase. He was a Frisbee pro—a veteran of San Diego beaches and Ivy League campuses—and made a long, graceful lunge, picking the disk neatly out of midair. It dawned on me that this might be the ticket.

I found a roll of duct tape under the seat of my pickup and, out of Jake's sight, taped the partridge to the top of the Frisbee. Then, in my most affected voice, I encouraged Jake in his excitement. I held the Frisbee above him with the partridge safely on top and out of sight. He again leaped and yipped. When I sent the disk wobbling out into the grass, he charged after it as usual. But when he came close he jumped back like he'd found a rattlesnake. Still, he knew the Frisbee was there and wanted badly to bring it back. He sat down and studied the problem. Finally, he reached out and, with lips curled delicately back, took the edge of the Frisbee in his teeth and dragged the whole works back to lay at my feet. Never did he, in any way, come in contact with the bird.

We had to start with a single tail feather taped to the Frisbee and work up through two feathers, a wing, two wings, and eventually a whole bird. But in a week he was over his dread of birds. I had to tape a pigeon's wings to its sides to get Jake to start putting moving birds in his mouth, but when he figured out what I wanted, he was a natural. In no time he was making seventy-five-yard, blind retrieves and doing them with enthusiasm.

While all this was going on, I was getting Spud ready for his first exposure to pheasants. I didn't expect much from such a pup but figured him to put a few birds into the air. He was such a go-getter I was sure he would hunt hard. Unlike Jake, his problem would be overzealousness, and that was a good kind of problem to have. My fear was not only that Jake might not retrieve, but also that he would just stick close to Kris and not hunt at all. I was afraid he might decide he didn't go for this rowdy life and quit without giving it a chance. I was afraid he might influence Kris to do the same.

All experienced hunters know that bad days happen. You can't let them get you down. If a dog fouls up or you can't shoot well, put it behind you. Things will be better the next time. But a bad day could be fatal for a thirty-year-old, with high expectations, going hunting with her faithful house dog—both for the first time. If Kris's interest died, I knew my life would veer from its ideal path and I'd find myself hunting mostly alone.

The importance of the pheasant hunt took on cosmic proportions and by the time the day arrived I was a nervous wreck. I worried about Jake drawing a tough old rooster with only a broken wing for his first retrieve, I worried about Kris's shooting, I worried that I wouldn't be able to resist kibitzing.

By the time everything was ready it was late in the season and the wild birds had been worked over pretty hard. In an effort to control some of the variables, I chose a hunting preserve for the outing. Twenty dollars a bird seemed awfully high but we were sure of birds and I reasoned that our team was not exactly a well-oiled hunting machine that could run up a huge bill.

The day dawned gray and the low, flat clouds threatened rain or worse. It was not the kind of day I'd hoped for and I offered up a little prayer to Orion as I loaded the dogs into their boxes. Kris was nearing the end of her residency and we had begun to talk about what might happen the next year. There were job opportunities in California, Chicago, about any big city, but she didn't want that. She had come to like South Dakota and thought she might like the kinds of things we were doing that day. I looked at the sky as we pulled into the shooting preserve. There was a faint streak of blue directly overhead, but the horizon was still chalky and snow was still a possibility.

We drove to a half section of thick bromegrass with old, weedy milo fields along the edge of standing corn. There was a marshy spot where cattails grew thick below a large stock dam, from which we heard the sounds of geese and mallards. We unloaded near the corn and headed along the milo. I carried a gun but wasn't out to shoot. I hoped Spud would find a bird or two and maybe flash-point one. What I was really there for was to see to it that Kris had a good time.

It got off to a bad start. A rooster jumped at her feet before we were thirty yards from the truck and she fired twice before the gun touched her shoulder. She shot fifteen feet over the bird. Jake didn't flinch at the shots but didn't pay much attention to the bird, either. Spud chased it out of sight.

While we waited for the little imp to return, I tried to keep Kris's mood light. But she's a competitive person and was used to breaking clay pigeons. She was instantly angry at herself—a beginner's mistake—and I was afraid it would affect her whole day. I seldom care if a bird comes to bag, but that day it seemed crucial. I laughed it off: "Everyone misses, forget it. Take your time. You've got lots of time." And the more I talked, the more I knew it was the wrong thing to do. I had to force myself to shut up. We waited in silence and Jake lay down at Kris's feet. When Spud finally returned, Jake got up and sniffed at the huffing little pup as if to ask what the big deal was.

We set off again, walking along the edge of the cattails, and the sky began to clear. The winter browns went rich with shadow and we both praised the changing weather. Suddenly it was pleasant just walking there with Kris. This was more what I'd hoped for. Spud was somewhere in the next county but I wasn't going to let that spoil the day. Jake pottered ahead, and it was possible that he might stumble onto a pheasant. Kris and I were both beginning to enjoy the day when Spud angled in from outer space and flushed a rooster twenty-five yards to our left. It was one of those tough, long, crossing shots. I didn't even pull up on it. But Kris brought her gun up and poked a shot. I winced when I saw the gun barrel stop just before she shot. The bird was forty yards out and going forty miles an hour by then. She missed it by a mile. "You got to keep the gun moving," I said before I thought to say it diplomatically.

Kris frowned. "I don't know about this," she said. It was in the tone of voice I had dreaded for weeks. I felt a touch of panic. It was me. I was driving her crazy.

"Look," I said. "Spud is running amok. I'm going to take him up into that bromegrass, where I can keep an eye on him. You and Jake walk up to the dam, then back through the cattails. There should be birds in the cattails for sure."

I gathered Spud up and headed out. I figured the only chance was to leave her alone and hope the improving weather would work its magic. As I started uphill toward the brome bench I saw Jake watching me. He looked from me to Kris and back again. At the time I thought he was just confused about our splitting up. But over the years I came to realize that he sensed the tension in the air. Now, lying in that strange New Hampshire bed, it was clear to me that he had been evaluating things—trying to understand what was at stake.

Once Spud and I were alone, the day won me over. As soon as I started to concentrate on the puppy, everything mellowed out. He was wearing down and I stayed on him until he was quartering in front of me fairly well. We worked up through the brome for a few minutes and he bumped a hen. But he seemed to hesitate just before the bird took to the air and only chased it a few yards. After we made the turn and started back, he hit scent and stopped. He held it until I was in range. When it came up, I killed Spud's first bird.

We celebrated with a good petting in the dry grass and for an instant I forgot about Kris and Jake. But when we got walking again, the nagging feeling in the back of my head was still there. When we came to where we could look down on the cattail slough I was holding my breath, hoping Kris and Jake were not back at the pickup.

But they were still hunting the cattails. I resisted the temptation to join them. Spud and I sat down in the golden grass above them. It only took an instant to see that they really didn't know where to look for birds. They wandered to areas that seldom hold them. It was all I could do not to shout directions from the hill. But Jake was out front, quartering within range, and they looked happy enough. Spud was on a lead then and we settled in to watch the woman I love work her first cattail slough with her pet retriever. I was afraid it might be her last, but they didn't look too bad. Their demeanor had changed since I last saw them. They were concentrating on what they were doing, yet somehow casual and relaxed. Something magic had happened in my absence. There was an ease and excitement in Kris's walk I hadn't noticed before, but have seen a thousand times since.

They were certainly pushing birds in front of them. The way they were working the slough, they might just run into a herd of them where the cattails ended. There was a particular corner of firebush that looked good to me and Jake was leading Kris right to it.

I sat up a little as they approached the firebush. Jake's gait picked up. His tail was ringing! He began to bounce and up came a bird. Bang—and it folded. I couldn't believe it. It was beautiful. Jake charged into the brush and brought the bird to Kris. I could hear her whoop with delight.

But Jake didn't bask in the praise. He spit the bird into Kris's hand and dived back into the bushes. Up came another pheasant. Bang. Another perfect retrieve. Back into the bushes. Two birds. Bang. Bang. Kris stopped to reload as Jake searched out the birds.

Then birds were coming up everywhere. Bang! Bang! She had two more down before the rocketing pheasants turned into twenty-dollar bills in my mind. I struggled to my feet. "Wait."

By the time I'd hustled down the hill with Spud straining on the lead ahead of me, Kris had eight birds lined up on the ground. The gun was empty and she was kneeling with her arms around a panting, very happy retriever. She beamed up at me and I beamed back.

For weeks afterward all Kris could talk about was how great the hunt had been. Winter set in with a vengeance then and we didn't get a chance to hunt again that year. But Kris was hooked deep, and as a result we've spent hundreds of days in the field since. That first hunt became part of our history, part of what makes us what we are, part of what had led us to that rented house in New Hampshire.

Not long after that first hunt, old Morgan died, and though you always take the death of a dog hard, we knew it was his time and he'd had a good, full life. The real shock came early that spring, just after Kris and I decided to make our relationship official. It was the spring of Kris's last year of residency and we planned to get married and live in the Black Hills.

Jake had not been his old self for a couple of days, so we took him for a checkup. The vet wanted to keep him overnight for some tests. We really didn't think much about it. But early in the morning—it was a Sunday, because Kris was home—he called to say that Jake had died.

Kris was speechless and handed the phone to me. I listened dumbfounded while this perfectly nice young vet tried to explain. He was very upset and obviously had no idea what had really happened. I listened to him rattle on, searching for the explanation he never found. The cause of death was unknown. But I knew instantly why Jake was dead. It all fell into place for me and the knowledge of it has shaped my life.

Jake died because his job was done. He'd seen Kris through medical school, her internship, and her residency. He'd been there through rough and lonely times. He'd helped transform her from a college girl to a woman. He'd led her through a cattail slough and into a flock of pheasants. He'd eased her into a new, more vital life and he was counting on me to take it from there.

It was a terribly sad time in our lives. Most of the day I held Kris, rocked her, and tried my best to make her see what Jake had given her. But his gifts weren't only for Kris.

Lying in that New Hampshire bed I couldn't help thinking that I might be letting Jake down. He would not have left Kris alone. Every time I closed my eyes I saw his big square head, and the wisdom in his face was haunting.

But the falcons had to be released in less than forty-eight hours. If I lingered even a couple of days they would be too mature to stick around the hacksite long enough to learn the terrain. They might simply bolt from the box and never return. I had created other responsibilities for myself. The falcons and the dogs were counting on me.

First
Frost

Summer dawns come early on the Northern Plains. To beat the sun a person has to be up by four o'clock. My flight was late the night before so I didn't get back to the ranch until nine in the evening. Then Erney spent a couple of hours getting me caught up on what was happening. I ended up with only five hours of sleep. Luckily, I'd slept well on the airplane, but it wouldn't have mattered. As I waited for the coffee to perk and watched the eastern sky lighten, I felt completely wide awake and fine-tuned to what was about to happen.

Erney came through the front door just as I poured my first cup. Moose had been running up and down the stairs with a ball in her mouth for twenty minutes and happened to be just starting down when the door opened. She sailed off the stairs with ears flying and landed in Erney's arms. Erney took it in stride. "Morning, Moosey." She licked his beard and wiggled free. It was still early for Mel and Spud but they raised their heads and whacked the floor a couple of times with their tails. I poured a cup for Erney and we settled in to wait for the sun and to go over our game plan for the falcons' release.

Opening the hackbox is a serious matter. The birds were forty-two days old, as close to the natural day of fledging as we could get. They had been paddling their wings inside the box for nearly a week now. Almost all the white down had disappeared from the tops of their heads and there was a distant, wild look in their eyes.

Baby falcons are like baby people; at certain ages they do certain things. There are individual differences but falcons don't fly at thirty-five days any more than babies walk at four months. They go on their first soar at about fifty days; they make their first kill at about seventy. Some, of course, are faster learners than others. One of the objects of hacking birds is to find the bird that, if it were human, would read Chekhov, in Russian, at five years old.

SOAR. The nearly effortless flight of a falcon or hawk achieved by the use of air currents. Once the technique is mastered, birds can stay up very high for hours with only occasional wing flapping.

But first they have to be released. I took the dogs for a good long run so they were tired when they were put into the kennel. We wanted them out of the way for the whole day. The worst possible thing to happen on the day of release is for a falcon to be frightened off the box. If the birds have a chance to come out, eat, look around, and leave the box in their own time, they almost always come back. Some birds stay on the box for two days before they make their first flight, and that is the very best situation. But if a bird is flushed from the box, by a clumsy person, a hungry eagle, or a curious puppy, it may fly straight away and not come down until it's somewhere over the state of Tennessee. The chores were done and Dundee and Little Bird, who were now nearly through with their annual molt, were fed so we wouldn't have to worry about them for the day. By eight o'clock we were ready.

There is a reverence that surrounds a falcon release. It is a rite of passage, a solemn initiation, a sort of falcon bar mitzvah without the party. It is not something to be done roughly or without ritual. I crept up the ladder to the hackbox without making a sound. Our box is rigged with a divider that can be lowered slowly to confine the falcons to the west side of the box while a small release door is taken off the east side. Defrosted pigeons can be spread out on the east side of the box so, when the divider is raised again and the falcons are free to leave via the release door, their attention is diverted from the blue sky and freedom by fresh food. Erney had been lowering and raising the divider for days now, so they were used to being crowded to one side of the box. Before I did anything to disturb the falcons, I took a couple of minutes to have a good look at them in a completely relaxed state. Once the door was opened it would be too late to change course. Any imperfection or injury would condemn them to a grisly death.

The tiercel wore a white band and, because males mature earlier, looked older than the falcons. He had no down left. His back was nearly black and the vertical streaks on his breast were fine where they melted into the buff of his neck. His head was a black helmet and his eyes were as big and deep as bullet holes. The falcon with the yellow band still had three puffs of down on her head that made her look funny, but was a good-sized bird and I guessed she'd fly at thirty-four ounces. Generally speaking, the bigger the better, but I've found that it's the size of a bird's heart that really matters, and that's hard to judge when you're peeking through a quarter-inch hole in a piece of plywood.

The "red" falcon was the one that grabbed me when she went into the box. She, too, had a bit of down on her head, but somehow she didn't look comical as did her sister. Like the other birds, her

HARD PENNED. The culmination of feather growth, when the feather reaches full length and the nourishing blood inside the quill dries, leaving the feather hard and complete.

wing feathers were short; the last primaries still had an inch or so to grow before the blood that nourishes the feather would dry in the shaft and the birds would be hard penned. She stood on a rock the size of a big grapefruit, her tail just touching the gravel of the box floor. She stared out across the prairie as if she were seething inside, angry that her primaries were not yet ready to take her to the horizon.

When I was satisfied that they were ready to go, I lowered the divider and reached down for the screw gun and plastic bag of pigeon that Erney handed up to me. I scurried up onto the top of the weathering yard and began scattering parts of pigeons where the birds would find them when they emerged. Erney had withheld a day's worth of food from the falcons, so eating would be foremost in their minds. I tossed a few pigeon quarters in front of the box and tied some to the top so they couldn't be carried or blown away. Then I took the small plywood door off with the screw gun and scattered more pigeon parts inside, on the floor of that part of the box from which the falcons were now excluded. When the divider was raised, the first thing the birds would see would be their meal, right where they were used to eating it. They wouldn't see the doorway to the great outdoors until they had started eating.

The hackbox and the release procedure were designed to ease the falcons into their new freedom. If everything is done right, there is little chance a bird will bolt from the box and be prematurely airborne. There are many things about a hack that cannot be controlled, but if it is to be successful, everything that can be controlled must be. So after I made everything ready and Erney had taken up his post at the spotting scope set up at the kitchen window, I sat for an extra few minutes making sure the birds were completely relaxed before I began slowly to raise the divider.

Erney had done a good job. The falcons paid no attention to the moving divider but jumped immediately to their food. I sneaked down the ladder and ran around the barn and shop in a wide loop that brought me to the front of the house without being seen from the hackbox. I came through the front door and up behind Erney, who was glued to the spotting scope. "How're we doing?"

"So far, fine as frog hair. They're all eating away. White looked out the door a couple of times but he's back to eating."

"Excellent." I jotted down what he told me in the logbook. "Time for more coffee," I said, and had almost reached the pot when Erney called out.

"There he is."

I grabbed my binoculars and twisted the tiercel into focus. He balanced on the perch just inside the box that served as the release door's sill. He looked out over the wire top of the weathering yard and bobbed his head at another perch set up four feet in front of him. The doorway he stood in was made to be too small for the falcons to fly through. They had to at least hesitate before they launched into the world. Our hope was that they would simply jump out onto the weathering yard and explore that area before actually flying. We had never had a bird blow out, and the white tiercel was no exception. He teetered there on the door perch for a minute, then jumped down to the top of the weathering yard. He ran across the wire toward the perch. There was a pigeon breast on the perch and he jumped up and footed it. He tried to stay on the perch but fell the eight inches back down. He dragged the pigeon with him and, though he looked indignant, began pulling feathers as if he'd planned to fall off the perch. "Yes," I said. "One down, two to go."

An hour later the yellow falcon appeared at the doorway. She looked to the sky, then down at the tiercel, who had finished eating. He gripped the top of the weathering yard and flapped his wings furiously. This is a sort of falcon flight simulator and it must have looked like fun to the yellow falcon, because she tried to spread her own wings. But the doorway was too narrow and she fell out and into a heap beside the fascinated tiercel. They both began flapping like mad but didn't move more than an inch.

"Two down, one to go," Erney said. And just then the tiercel let go and elevated a foot off the wire and began to paddle for the house. The other two birds and the old falcons in their molting chambers began to cheer him on with wild kakking. He came right at us and I thought he would crash into the wall beside the window. But he pulled up and went out of our sight. I ran to the front door and watched to see if he would keep going toward the south. I saw nothing but a thousand miles of blue sky and the Black Hills below.

When I crept out and looked up at the roof, there he was, as high as he could get, majestically preening his feathers, straightening things up after his first flight. "All right," Erney said when I gave him the news. He jotted it in the log. "First flight."

Then the sun got high, the wind tapered off, the temperature soared. The midday doldrums set in and nothing moved. It is the natural order of things to take a long break in the middle of the day. In a prairie summer, when the hot days stretch to eighteen hours, all the action in the real world takes place in the morning and the evening. If you plan to take part in that action, it only makes sense to rest up in the middle of the day.

Erney and I alternated snoozing and watching the hack. But the birds were snoozing too, so there wasn't much to watch until four o'clock, when the yellow falcon hopped to a piece of pigeon and started to pull at a tough wing butt. The tiercel had been on the house all day and I hoped he would stay put—where we could keep an eye on him—until the next day. But when the falcon began to pull feathers and let them float off into the wind, the tiercel went back to the hackbox and landed like an old pro. This was great. The biggest hurdle in a hack is getting the birds back to the box for the first time. After that, they come and go readily. The tiercel was on his way.

The two birds played tug-of-war with the pigeon for nearly an hour. During this time, the red falcon peered out of the door and we were sure she'd come out soon. In fact, at seven o'clock, after the other two birds had succeeded in tearing the pigeon to shreds and they each stood on one leg in the angling sun with full crop and drooping eyelids, Red suddenly appeared in the doorway. I called to Erney, who was at the stove making some of his special beans and hamburger goulash. "Here she comes," I said.

This should have been the perfect first day of hack. The sun was on the way down, one bird had flown and returned, and it looked like we'd put them all to bed safe and sound on the platform just outside the hackbox. But Red did not jump down the way we hoped. She glared cautiously to her left and right, then spun with an excited kak and leaped back into the box.

"What the . . . ?" Erney never got the chance to finish. Another bird shot in from the east and grabbed a pigeon leg. The two falcons who were outside jumped into the air and paddled frantically for the northern horizon. I kept my eye on them. The tiercel curved and made a southerly loop. That was good. He would come down in sight of the house that he already knew. But the yellow falcon, flying in jerks and starts, disappeared over the hill a quarter of a mile to the north.

"Oh shit," I said. "What was it?"

"That damned Cooper's hawk," Erney said. "It's just a stupid lost baby. I figured it starved to death. I haven't seen it for five days."

"Well, it's not hard to see now." I picked up the binoculars and focused them on the top of the hackbox. It was a Cooper's hawk, all right, but I couldn't tell the sex. It stood on the hackbox clutching the pigeon part. After watching the peregrines all day this bird seemed misshapen. Its head was small, its legs grossly long, and its wing tips touched high on its back instead of crossing over the tail like a falcon's. Its tail was twice as long as a falcon's—a rudder made for tight turns. In the binoculars, the Coop's eyes were intense, desperate, and thoroughly insane. If Jack the Ripper could fly, he would look like a Cooper's hawk. This bird gazed down at the feathers and meat in its talons as if it just remembered what it was doing. Then it footed the bundle madly, as if to kill it again, and flew off so fast that it was behind the barn in an instant.

"We got big problems," I said. "Red is scared but safe. White's been out and back. He'll probably be back. But Yellow might still be flying."

"And she's the slowest of the lot," Erney said.

There was only an hour and a half left before sunset and not much we could do. I left Erney at the spotting scope and went out the front door with my binoculars in hand. Almost as soon as I left the yard I saw the tiercel sitting on the cab of the tractor parked on the edge of the field of CRP grass just to the west of our buildings. He looked a little jumpy, so I swung around him in a hundred-yard arch and up the hill to the ridge where Yellow was last seen.

CONSERVATION RESERVE PROGRAM (CRP). The Department of Agriculture program that promotes seeding marginal farmland back to grass. The CRP is responsible for a huge increase in wildlife populations.

That ridge is a divide; the land falls off to the south and the north. The north side runs down in rough woody draws and finally drains into Whitewood Creek a few miles to the northwest. It's a huge, wild area with no sign of humanity and the known haunt of a half-dozen different kinds of predators. I'd seen many coyotes and foxes from the ridge, wild falcons and hawks used the small buttes that rise up on the east edge for hunting perches, but the most ominous feature is the stand of ash and cottonwoods around the draws. Great horned owls lurk in places like that, and they are deadly to young falcons. This is very dangerous territory for a young, uncoordinated falcon to spend a night.

I wanted to walk those draws and try to locate her. She was likely sitting confused on the ground, about as vulnerable as she could be. If I could find her, I could spend the night close by and maybe ward off the predators. But the sun was going down and she would be very hard to see. I could walk up too close to her in the poor light and frighten her more than she already was.

I was heartsick as I retraced my arch around the tiercel. His silhouette stood out against the pink sunset and his posture showed me that he had settled in for the night. The lights came on in the house just as I got to the site of the partridge building we planned to start construction on soon. It was just about in the center of the homestead. I looked around at this hard country and thought, "This whole place is temporary." In that falling light the gnarled grove looked like something from the *Wizard of Oz*. The shop and house found a shade of pink in the sunset and reflected it at me. I thought of the baby falcon huddled on a hillside and imagined the hollow hoot of a great horned owl. The night was starting to cool off and I shivered.

I knew it was going to be a long night. There wouldn't be much sleep no matter what I did, so after we ate some of Erney's goulash and he went back to his cabin, I took my sleeping bag and made my way through the dark, knee-high grass back to the top of the ridge. I rolled the bag out somewhere between the tiercel and the lost falcon. My presence would have no effect on the falcon's fate, but being there, giving up a little comfort for her sake, made me feel better. I lay in the grass and watched the stars. There were millions of them and when they came into focus, all my senses became acute. I could have heard an owl hoot a mile away.

The tiercel came in to eat at six-thirty the next morning. The sight of him playing with his food brought the red falcon to the doorway. She scowled at the tiercel for only a few seconds, then jumped to take his food away. He hopped back, then reached out and tugged on the pigeon a couple of times. But the falcon had not eaten the night before and wasn't going to give it up. The tiercel found another piece of pigeon and by ten-thirty they both stood asleep, with full crops, in the shade of the hackbox. The yellow falcon did not show up.

We watched all day from the house. We had planned to take up the two older falcons that morning. For the next week we would be mostly confined to the house and it would be a good time to carry the birds on our fists and reclaim them for the coming hunting season. But the fact that Yellow was not back took the wind out of our sails; it was late afternoon before we got everything organized.

The mews is really the east side of the shop. It's a metal building fifty feet by twenty-five feet and stands seventy feet west of the house. The falcons' part of the building consists of three rooms, each ten feet wide and fifteen feet long. The first room has an eight-foot ceiling with two workbenches, a cupboard, and a screen perch along one whole wall. This is where the birds stay at night when they're in training and where we keep equipment like jesses, hoods, blocks, bells, bags, telemetry equipment, and gloves. The other two rooms are molting chambers, with ceilings clear to the roof of the building, fifteen feet

TAKE UP. To begin the training of an intermewed or hacked falcon or hawk. Also, to first get a bird on the fist.

RECLAIM. The term has come to mean the retraining of an intermewed falcon or hawk but used to refer to the training of any class of falcon or hawk.

SCREEN PERCH. A long perch used to keep falcons, and occasionally hawks, at night. A cloth screen hangs below the perch so the bird cannot go under and get tangled. These perches are not safe unless the birds are healthy and used to them.

JESS. The leather strap between the bracelets and the swivel.

high. The molting chambers have pea-rock floors and perches screwed to the walls. Dundee and Little Bird had each been free in a room since February. Now, in late July, their feathers were ready for the new hunting season that would open the first of September.

Some falcons get extremely wild during their molt and, because familiarity with people sometimes breeds contempt, they act worse than fresh-caught birds when you take them up to be reclaimed. One approach is just to go into the chamber, catch them, jess them, hood them, and put them on a perch until they remember that they are noble hunting hawks. This works, all right, but we take a slightly different tack. About two weeks before they are to be taken up, we start reducing their food rations. They are always terribly fat from the season of high rations and inactivity. They need to lose weight anyway; by doing it slowly, we eliminate any undue stress. Reducing their food gets them interested in us again. They start looking forward to feeding time, and with every feeding we spend more time in the chamber with them. By the time the big day comes, they are well on their way to being reclaimed. But depending on how much weight they have lost, the rest of the job could take another week or two. It's almost always a month before they can fly with any authority.

We started with Dundee because he was about the friendliest falcon on the planet. I went to work building a leather bewit with which to attach the bell and name tag to his leg, while Erney went into the chamber with hood, jesses, and food. I expected it to take ten minutes for Dundee to come to Erney's fist, but he was back in two. Erney hadn't even hooded him. Dundee acted like he had never been put up to molt. He stood on Erney's fist pulling on the

BEWIT. The leather strap that holds an accessory (bell, name tag, radio transmitter) to the leg of a falcon or a hawk.

tiring and paid no attention to me as I fastened the bell to his leg. When he finished eating, Erney slipped the hood on his head with no fuss and put him on the scale. Nineteen ounces.

TIRING. A tough piece of food given to a falcon or hawk. A tiring is usually given while the bird is on the fist to prolong the positive association with the falconer.

"An ounce over flying weight," I said. "Good work." Erney grinned as he tied Dundee on the screen perch. He had made the decisions on lowering the birds' weight and he was proud of himself for guessing Dundee's weight just right.

As soon as he brought Little Bird out I could see at a glance that she had tricked him. She likes Erney and so had come down to the fist. But when she saw me, her eyes got big as quarters and her feathers slicked down for action. She paid no attention to the pigeon wing at her feet. When I picked up her bell, she acted like it was a tennis racket. She bated hard off Erney's fist and hit the end of her jesses like a roped calf. She kakked and spun and flailed the air with her wings. "Looks like she remembers you," Erney said.

She has always been obtuse with me and I like to blame it on her species. She is from Iraq—if she had been a tiercel I would have named her Saddam. This behavior was typical for her when she was fat. When we got the hood on her and got her quieted down, I bet with Erney: "Five bucks says she weighs twenty-three ounces." That was four ounces over her flying weight, as much as we had ever known her to weigh.

"No way," said Erney. "She's been sweet as a puppy."

"To you, maybe. But you know she's a sandbagging harlot." My feelings and pride were still hurt from a trip to Washington state the winter before, where Little Bird had humiliated me in front of falconer friends by refusing to stoop at partridge flushed under her.

She'd flown high but her temperamental personality had nearly ruined the two-thousand-mile trip. "Put her on the scale," I said.

I could see the needle pointing way above her flying weight of
nineteen ounces, but I stood back and let Erney read it. He dug his bent
and scratched half glasses from his coverall pocket, hung them on his
nose, and leaned down to look. He froze in that position for a few seconds, then jiggled the scale and looked again. "Well, kiss my ass," he said.

It was a new world record for a Barbary falcon—twenty-six
and a half ounces. We tied her on the screen perch beside Dundee. It
was going to be a long time until she'd be ready to fly free. When we
stepped out of the mews, the first thing we saw was a flash of brown.
"Oh, no," Erney said. The falcons on the hackbox started kakking
wildly and the tiercel took to the air just as the Cooper's hawk landed
on the box. The red falcon was on the opposite corner and when she
spread her wings I cringed. But she didn't take off as her sister had.
With wings outspread and head down, she charged the Cooper's hawk.

I thought she made a terrible mistake, but she knew what
she was doing. She closed with the intruder and suddenly the
Cooper's hawk looked much smaller. It squeaked and tried to fly, but
Red leaped into air, raking her feet like a fighting cock. Feathers scattered from the Coop's chest. "All right!" Erney cheered. "Get that
beady-eyed little varmint!"

Finally the Coop pulled away and beat a hard retreat around
the barn. Red almost went after it but, just in time, remembered that
she didn't know how to fly. Her feathers stayed puffed as she paced
back and forth on top of the box. "Maybe that's the end of it," Erney
said. But we both knew it wasn't likely.

The last few hours of the second night of the hack were busy.
The tiercel came and went a couple of times and the red falcon made

her first flight. She got as far as the top of one of the partridge pens behind the barn. She was in sight of the hackbox, so it was a good place for her to spend the night. She paid no attention to the partridge hiding below and began to preen the last of the down out of her tail.

We didn't talk about it, but we knew the chances of seeing Yellow again diminished with every hour. We ate what was left of the hamburger-bean goulash and stared out the window toward the north. At seven-thirty we left the house, which had been serving as our blind, and moved onto the deck. We kept our movements slow so as not to frighten the falcons. We drank beer and talked about the Cooper's hawk. Neither of us knew much about them. Though some people fly them, we never had. Erney made a big point out of saying he never had the desire, while I thought their short-winged sprinter's approach to predation was fascinating. They are about the opposite of a peregrine falcon. They catch birds like a peregrine but do it in short bursts of speed, often in close cover. They are hawks for the bush; falcons are open-country birds.

Erney thought our Cooper's hawk was a female and I thought it might be a male. I dragged a book out and learned they weigh less than they look, a female around a pound and a male close to twelve ounces. Because our Coop was built so much differently from the falcons we were used to, we couldn't even guess its weight. We discussed all this in an effort to forget that Yellow was still out. Every time we stopped talking, a heavy stillness settled over the whole ranch.

When Erney went to his cabin and left me alone, the stillness turned to sadness. A hack can go to pieces in a hurry, and with one bird already missing and a Cooper's hawk marauding the box, things did not look good. It was possible that in two days all the birds would be gone and my equinox autumn would fail before it had really begun. I sat at the picnic table with the last of the sunlight slanting across the prairie and sending spikes of shadow out behind every blade of grass. The tiercel came back to the box again and began to pull on a pigeon foot—a snack before bed. The evening was calm and melancholy.

Then there was a streak of movement and a chorus of kakking. I was on my feet. This time I wasn't going to worry about frightening the falcons. It was risky but I'd had it with this Cooper's hawk. I'd simply chase the damned thing away. I started off the deck, expecting the tiercel to take to the air in front of the oncoming bird. But he didn't move. He kakked and bowed, and I knew the streak I'd seen was not the Coop. It was Yellow!

She sailed in and landed as though she'd been doing it for years. She hadn't eaten for over a day and grabbed a piece of meat like her life depended on it. She began eating so furiously that she didn't notice me, frozen in stride, exposed halfway between the house and the hackbox.

I couldn't move. Frightening the tiercel was one thing, he had been out and back a half-dozen times, but if Yellow noticed me there, just thirty feet away, she might bolt into the night and be lost for good. I did my best Marcel Marceau imitation, moving only my head so I could see the setting sun. It would touch the horizon in twenty minutes. The light would linger for another hour. It was a piece of cake. I could stand there all night if I had to.

We settled into a routine. I was up by four-thirty, when the air still held the crispness of night. The three dogs were loaded into the pickup as the sky began to lighten. By the time the sun actually made its appearance above the eastern ridges, Spud and Mel were running in sharptail country and Moose was waiting her turn in the truck kennel. It was still too early in the season to find broods easily. Game birds are uncanny in their ability to stay hidden when the chicks are still small. In summer it often seems like there are no birds around; then one day in late August there are birds everywhere. These early-morning sessions were mostly conditioning. Spud and Mel occasionally found a bird and I encouraged them to point and hold, but mostly I wanted them to run.

After the setters were worn out—and that didn't take long—it was Moose-Anne's turn. We went to our alfalfa field, where the vegetation had been cut close earlier in the year. It was a big, open area where she could see the retrieving dummy when I tossed it. She was just a pup, so this was mostly play. She loved it. Her secondary job would be to walk at heel when Kris and I were bird hunting and retrieve downed birds. Her first job was to put up birds for the falcons. This needs to be done with precision, so the training sessions concentrated on going to a spot on command. It wasn't long before Moose figured out that hand signals would lead her to the retrieving dummy, and she thought that was a pretty good deal. Later, I would substitute a pigeon for the dummy. The goal was to be able to direct her, from fifty yards up-wind, to a place I had seen birds land. If I could get her there at exactly the right instant, the falcon who would tend to wait on over me would have the wind at her back when she stooped. But all that was a ways off for Moosey. On those first mornings it was enough to keep her focused: simple retrieves, no butterfly chasing, no gopher excavating.

By the time I made it back to the house, Erney had finished the chores. The pigeons, chickens, and partridge had been fed. The kennels were clean, the water bowls filled. The coffee was on and the food for the hack birds was thawing in the sink. Either Little Bird or Dundee was on Erney's fist as he waited for the first hack bird to come in.

They usually came about eight o'clock and sat on the buildings or on the telephone poles. The Cooper's hawk was still around, but after Red had shown her whose hackbox it was, she mellowed out. Occasionally we saw her sitting calmly not five feet from a falcon. We still weren't sure what sex it was so we started calling it Alice Cooper's hawk.

CHIP. A soft vocalization of a friendly and contented falcon.

RING UP. To ascend, usually by circling and usually in an effort to get above another bird.

The pigeons were let out of the loft about nine and we watched to see how the falcons reacted. Nothing happened the first few days. They twisted their heads and occasionally chipped as the homers circled and rang up, but they didn't chase them. The tiercel was the first to show interest, and in another day all three birds would take long, playful runs at the pigeons from the tops of power poles. When everyone was in the air or off on the high-line poles a quarter mile south, we would put the food out. The falcons weren't always hungry, so sometimes it took an hour or two for them to come for the food. Eventually they ate and Erney and I would carefully note in the log how each bird acted.

By then it would be noon, and after a little lunch things would slow in the heat of the day. The first week, while the dogs and hawks slept, I busied myself with designing and laying out the new partridge building. For years Erney and I had been experimenting with ways to ensure that we always had flights for the falcons. It's a big problem in falconry. Falcons are athletes and like any other athlete they need rigorous training if they're going to excel. However, the skills learned on the lure or pigeons do not transfer well to game birds. You can make a fair game hawk in many ways, but a really great one needs to fly at its intended quarry hundreds and hundreds of times.

Some years that is not a problem. Some years finding a good slip can take hours and that won't work; the nature of the Great Plains is even more cyclic than in other places. The obvious solution is to release game birds to supplement the natural production. But the art of game-bird releasing is crude. There have been some decent results with pheasants for gun hunters, but a bird that gets shot never has the chance really to use its powers of flight. There is no evasive maneuvering when a pheasant is shot. It flies straight and it either comes down or it gets away. When a wild bird is chased by a falcon, it does things that gun hunters never see. The best quarry can sideslip, duck, flap a wing in the falcon's face, change speeds, bail out, even do barrel rolls. Released birds do none of these things. These feints and ploys have either been bred out of them or require months of free flying to be developed. Most released birds are wholly unsatisfactory for falconry: They're much too easy to catch, or they refuse to fly at all.

SLIP. A chance to catch quarry.

In the mid-eighties we imported Hungarian partridge eggs from Denmark. We hatched them in an incubator and tried to raise them. Huns pair up; you can't just put a few in a pen and collect eggs. The females are particularly aggressive and will kill rival suitors. It was not an easy task but we managed to raise enough birds to try our release scheme. We built big, permanent recall pens on

RECALL PEN. A secure wire cage built so that game birds can get into it but cannot get out unless released by a person.

the edges of stubble fields and put twenty birds in each pen. We let ten birds out every day to give them maximum conditioning. It took years to figure out just how to train them to return and how to keep them from getting eaten by predators but we finally got so we could, with falcons, harvest about fifty percent of what we put out. They flew well and held for dogs just like wild birds do. The discriminating eye, though, could see that they still didn't have the moves of truly wild birds.

At the same time, we experimented with letting parents incubate and raise their own broods. This was even more difficult because each pair needed a large, safe, isolated pen that was protected from foul spring weather. But when it worked, it worked well. We released whole broods in various places and the adults took good care of the young. In winter there might be four groups of twelve captive raised birds around the ranch. But the way they were raised and released made a difference. Except for leg bands, they were indistinguishable from wild ones. The latest stage in the quest to stabilize our game population was a fifty- by twenty-foot partridge brood–rearing building.

We had been talking about it for years. Our design evolved into a long metal roof covering two rows of six pens. Each pen would be both open to the elements yet under the roof and isolated from the next pen. It would be predator-proof and designed so the birds could be taken care of without undue exposure to people, farm machinery, and frolicking dogs. There would be water, electricity, and an isolated feed shed on one end. The plan was to raise broods, then transplant the entire family to a release pen from which the birds could be gently hacked into the wild.

It was a preposterous plan but this fall was my chance to do things I had dreamed of doing. Over the years, Erney and I spent weeks and drank at least ten thousand gallons of coffee while we discussed this building. We've built hundreds of things together but it's not easy to see how, given the differences in our philosophies of construction. For this reason, I hired a local crew to put up the shell of the building. Erney and I would build all the pens and do all the finish work. We vowed that all decisions would be made democratically and that an environment of compromise would reign.

In those first days of the hack we cleared the site, ditched in the water and electrical, and staked the building corners. We didn't knock ourselves out and it was pleasant working in the dry South Dakota heat. We kept Dundee and Little Bird blocked out where they would get reaccustomed to human activity. Dundee was tame and approaching flying weight, so he often sat unhooded. Little Bird, true to her reputation, was losing only an eighth of an ounce a day despite getting almost nothing to eat. She remained hooded most of the time but even bare-headed she sat very still, conserving every calorie in an effort to put off training as long as possible.

Occasionally a hack falcon would fly over and eye us or make a pass at the pigeons, but during the middle of the day everyone mostly slept. Since I was getting up with the sun like all the other animals, about noon I found myself running out of gas. I started taking a little nap in the afternoons, and I enjoyed the mornings and evenings even more.

The days passed pleasantly but the nights were lonely. After their evening run the dogs settled in, with Moose and Mel chewing on each other and Spud growling if they chewed on him. The hack birds took to roosting in a huge cottonwood a quarter of a mile down the main draw. They went to sleep early, some nights lining up, all

CADGE. A wooden frame perch used to carry falcons and hawks.

three together, on a big limb near the center trunk. At that stage of training, Dundee and Little Bird spent the nights perched on a cadge in the middle of the kitchen floor. The dogs moving around helped tame them, and in a few days they slept with their hooded heads behind their wings even with Moose-Anne leaping over them every couple of minutes.

Early in the evenings Erney retired to his cabin to watch television. I would drink a glass of whiskey and read. Sometimes I'd sit in the hot tub and watch the sky. Always, I wondered how Kris was doing. We talked on the phone when she wasn't at the hospital and more and more we looked forward to the New Brunswick trip, when we'd get to spend ten days together. That trip was still two months away when the hack birds began to soar.

Erney was watching the tiercel on a particularly warm morning. I was out with the dogs and had taken a few pigeons to introduce Moose to birds. Erney said the tiercel was just sitting on a telephone pole when he saw one of the pigeons coming home. He took off to intercept it, gave it a good scare, then set his wings and made a tight turn. He must have hit a tremendous thermal air current rising off the warming earth because Erney wrote in the log that he spiraled upward without flapping a wing and was out of sight in two minutes. From then on, all the falcons started going for soars as soon as the day warmed up. They hung above the ridge to the east of the house, playing on the wind that was reflected skyward by the contour of the land.

Erney and I sat at the picnic table with ten-power binoculars and watched them adjusting individual wing feathers as they felt for the best air. When they found what they needed, they would start upward, jockeying for position to make the first stoop on their hack-mates thousands of feet above. In the second week they would all spend hours aloft catching what we think were dragonflies. It happened much too high to see what they were catching but we watched them stoop a few feet and snatch something out of the air. Often they would disappear even in the binoculars. It was impossible not to wonder, each time, if they would make it back. They always did, though, at least twice a day, for breakfast and dinner.

For the first three weeks of hack, birds will come in to eat morning and evening. If the meals are there at the same time, it's easy to tell when the first bird misses a meal. That means it's getting more independent and that the time to take them up is approaching. Since we only wanted two birds back—one for us and one for Pete—we planned to take them up when the first one missed two meals in a row. When they decide to leave, they do it fast. Often you don't get a bird back if it misses two meals. In fact, you'd better get busy or you could lose the whole works.

All that was at least a week off. I started flying Dundee to the lure and could tell right away that he had not gotten any more ferocious during his molt. He had a nice, crisp wing beat but none of the gutsy daring in his stoops that is the hallmark of wild falcons or well-trained birds. It's a critical flaw in birds that have to make it on their own. He might well have been one of the eighty percent that would have been selected out of the population in the first year. He was fun to be around, though. Life was a lark for him, and not a meadowlark—when I flushed one while he was on the wing, he didn't even look at it.

Alice Cooper's hawk had become a fixture of the hack. It came in with the other birds to eat twice a day and put a little extra pressure on our stock of frozen chickens, quail, and pigeons. I counted what was left and saw that if Little Bird didn't get down to weight soon and start adding partridge to the larder, things could get tough before duck season began. But I had no need to worry; the Coop, who was older than the falcons, and from a more barbarous lineage, began taking things into its own hands. It was found one morning inside the pigeon loft, dining on one of Erney's prize squabs. Three more pigeons lay beheaded on the floor. It had come right in through the bobber door. Erney, who had been predicting this, caught it red-handed. He was not amused and trapped it in a corner of the loft.

"Guilty as a bed-pisser," he said as he held the Coop in my face.

It looked silly there in Erney's big hand. Its wings were hunched up in a shrug and its shape reminded me of an ice cream cone. It was not nearly as compact or noble-looking as a peregrine. It looked savage—a slightly deranged kind of hawk. "He's neat," I said. "Look at those eyes."

"Assassin eyes," Erney said. "And it's got to be a she. Seventeen ounces. I weighed her."

I reached up and felt her crop. "Deduct an ounce or two for pigeon meat and she's still too big to be a male. What do we do with her?"

"Is it against the law to put her in a gunnysack with a brick?"

"Forget it, she's still a raptor."

"Yeah, but not like a peregrine. She's more like a weasel."

"Forget it, Ern."

"How about a one-way ticket to somewhere far away?"

"Good thinking. I need to go to Rapid City. Thirty-five miles ought to do it."

Erney smiled and looked in Alice's wild eyes. "You're going to the big city, you snaky little bastard."

I wrapped her in a towel and drove her to Canyon Lake Park to teach a lesson to the hundreds of ducks who hang out there making a living mooching off humans. These ducks are fat and sloppy. They are devoid of the alertness that every self-respecting duck prides itself in, and they tick me off. I knew that Alice wouldn't catch one, but the ducks would certainly recognize her. I couldn't get these ducks off welfare but I could give them a Darwinian wake-up call.

I tucked Alice under my jacket and walked out toward the raft of ducks quacking and paddling madly to shore in hopes of a handout. I let them come. I might even have led them to believe that the bundle under the jacket was a loaf of bread. They hit the beach a hundred strong and waddled up the bank like mallard Jell-O. I waited until they surrounded me, until the stragglers were ashore and the most aggressive ones were nibbling obnoxiously on my pant legs. Then I took Alice out and let her unfold in my hands.

It was like a fire alarm went off: profound duck panic, the sound of quacks, and flaps, and stampeding webbed feet. Alice took one look at this and flew straight up. That forced any ducks that were trying to fly to change their minds and crash into the water, where their buddies were paddling like hell. They pushed a tidal wave ahead of them and Alice spiraled out of sight.

I laughed all afternoon as I went about my chores in Rapid City. I hadn't been to town for three weeks and little jobs had accumulated. It was after five o'clock by the time I got back to the ranch, and I expected to see the three falcons pulling happily on their evening meal. But as I eased the pickup to a stop, I saw four silhouettes on the hackbox. I was confused until I saw Erney standing on the deck with his arms crossed and his jaw set. I didn't need binoculars to know that the fourth bird was Alice.

Erney is a gentle man but he's no pacifist. To Erney, wild is wild and domestic is domestic; when Alice entered his pigeon loft, she crossed a sacred line. I had to plead for her.

Of course it was illegal to hurt Alice even if she was killing domestic livestock, so Erney's response was limited. It would take more than the loss of a few pigeons to push Erney to crime, but nothing was keeping him from minor acts of torment. The pigeon loft was locked. Alice's favorite perch, a particular branch of an ash tree at the back of the cattle lot, mysteriously disappeared. He tied a pillowcase to a pole and waved it in Alice's face every chance he got. But Alice didn't get the message.

"That feathered reptile is getting tamer," Erney said.

I couldn't resist needling him. "I think she likes you, Ern."

"Well, the feeling ain't mutual. She's a curse. We ought to trap her ass and take her to Montana."

"Grabbing her once she's in the pigeon loft is one thing. Trapping her on purpose is something else. We'd need a permit to do that."

"Then we should get one. It's no big deal. Just fill out a form, wait a few days, snag 'er and ship 'er off."

I told him not to get carried away. She was a week ahead of the falcons and she'd start killing wild birds soon. After that she'd head south for the winter. The big accipiter migration starts to push through South Dakota in mid-August. She should be leaving any day.

In fact, the lark buntings were already bunched up for passage and the blackbirds had long since vacated the shelter of the trees around the ranch house for parts unknown. I was flying Dundee in the mornings and finally beginning to fly Little Bird in the evenings. Our training ground is the big flat lowland to the west of the house that we call The Bottom, and early and late on summer days it's filled with the activity of prairie birds. I kept turning Dundee loose in the vicinity of doves in the hope that they would stimulate him. But although they froze when they saw him in the air, he paid almost no attention to them when I flushed them. I would usually end up tossing a pigeon for him and he would chase it with what seemed like all his might, but he almost never caught it.

PASSAGE. The trip of a migrating bird. A term describing a migrating bird, i.e., a passage falcon.

For years, performances like Dundee's fooled me. Falcons can give the impression of just barely missing their quarry. They make it look like they are giving the chase everything they have and that only the quarry's last-minute, heroic maneuver saved its life. Sometimes this is true, but more likely the falcon is just playing. Except in the case of the most difficult game, a well-conditioned and mentally squared-away falcon, given the right slip, will hit and usually catch its prey. The whole trick to falconry is making sure the bird is well conditioned, mentally ready, and given a good opportunity. That sounds easy but, in fact, is hard to achieve.

In Dundee's case, his mind was never right. He just loved to fly around looking good, and—to the untrained eye—he seemed the very essence of winged fury. When he saw a pigeon he rolled in a complete flip, changing direction in a wink. His wings would go double-time, so fast that he looked like a miniature fighter jet. Given any height advantage he could catch up to a pigeon in no time and he would strike with a vicious upward slice. But usually he would only dislodge a few feathers. He made it appear that the pigeon had narrowly escaped, but I knew he had let it go. He was tame in a way that is not good for a falcon; it was all play for him and watching him made me long for a bird who took life as seriously as a wild one would. Only a bird with the attitude of a wild falcon could perform at the level needed to catch wild prey consistently, and Dundee just didn't have it. But he was so much fun to fly that I was out every morning exercising him before the hack birds came in to eat.

It was the first week of August, three weeks into the hack. All three birds were coming and going freely. They had all missed a daily meal or two and were much more independent. We had started to think about bringing them in, but, since the longer the birds are at hack the better, we wanted to wait until the last minute. The ideal situation would be to bring them in the day before the first bird would leave, probably the day after the most mature bird starting killing on its own. The dynamics of a hack are not what might be expected. A twenty-day hack is not twice as good as a ten-day hack—it is ten times better. A twenty-four-day hack is a hundred times better. A thirty-day hack is a thousand times better. The last few days of a hack, when the birds are finally beginning to chase and perhaps kill wild birds, are far more important than the first few weeks. The fact that the last days are also the most risky, because the birds naturally leave an area when they start killing on their own, makes hacking a dicey game. It's best to have one more bird at hack than you plan to bring in. Since they mature at slightly different rates—the males first—one can disappear and still allow time to get the others in before they take off.

The last few days of a hack are a mind game. I wanted the birds to have the advantage of every possible minute of freedom, but my whole fall depended on getting a bird back to fly. The birds were not hanging around the place the way they had, but Erney and I often saw one as we worked on the partridge building or when we checked the cattle in a pasture a mile away. We studied their postures and the way they pursued pigeons and wild birds. They were still playing games, but their powers of flight were increasing greatly. They would chase each other for hours and drive other raptors—even eagles—out of their air space.

RAPTOR. Any bird of prey.

On the twenty-second day of the hack I was down on The Bottom, a mile and a half from the house, exercising Dundee and wondering when the first frost would come. The crispness in the air had me thinking about autumn. It was only a few weeks until the falconry season began. The ducks had apparently grown their flight feathers back in preparation for their migration; I'd seen a few skirting the horizon that morning when I stepped out to watch the sun come up. I had tossed Dundee a couple of pigeons and he had chased them, feathered them, and come back for me to throw another. He was being his usual self, flashy but harmless, and even the pigeons knew they were not in trouble. The third pigeon went out of my hand, saw Dundee above, flapped as if it were skipping, waited for the stoop, then rolled out as Dundee shot past a yard wide of the mark. The pigeon took a few more leisurely wing beats to ensure that he was well above Dundee, and lined out for home.

PITCH UP. To shoot back up after a stoop; a hunting maneuver that readies the falcon for a second stoop.

Dundee has a beautiful pitch up. He rides the momentum of the stoop in a vertical arc and watches over his shoulder as if expecting his quarry to fall out of the air from sheer fright. He almost never continues his pursuit, and that morning was no different. But it was fun to watch the pressure of the air vibrating his wing tips as he spread his sail and started back for another pigeon. Sometimes you can hear the wind through his feathers and that's what I thought I was hearing that morning. But when he turned and hung motionless, the sound was still there. It hissed and built like an oncoming jet. When I let my eyes leave Dundee and found the pigeon, a hundred yards away now, I realized exactly what it was.

The pigeon knew that sound, too, and came to life. It was the sound of a serious falcon stoop. A black streak blurred from above. No, three streaks. It was the sound of three falcons stooping. They plummeted out of a morning cloud—one, two, three—like spitfires over London. How high they were when the stoops began is hard to say but they were easily still over five hundred feet high when I found them. They came like lethal raindrops, weighted and falling. Falling, falling with folded wings, and the pigeon began its evasive moves.

It sideslipped toward a small group of dwarf cottonwoods, the only cover for a mile. The first falcon had already considered them. Her stoop was calculated to deny that option and the pigeon came back hard just in time to avoid a collision. The first falcon pitched up two hundred feet as the second turned the pigeon into the stoop of the third. Feathers flew, but the pigeon lost only a few feet of altitude. Soon all three falcons were above it again, and the pigeon had lost most of its speed. The only escape was the cottonwoods, and the pigeon bet the farm on his ability to make it.

The next set of stoops were flat but hard. This time all three falcons connected, feathers came off in billows, and the last falcon bound to the pigeon, taking it to the ground fifty yards short of the cottonwoods.

The whole flight had taken only a minute, but I felt drained. I'd never seen anything quite like it. I'd watched a wild pair of peregrines chase a cliff swallow in a huge canyon off Lake Powell but the stoops had been shorter, more calculated, and the swallow had escaped. This was something different. There had been a crazy, adolescent fervor that was the hallmark of first-year falcons competing to see who would carry the genes forward into time. I stood spellbound, overwhelmed by my luck at having seen what was surely the birds' first kill.

I snapped myself back. Where was Dundee?

When I looked, he was still above me, waiting on at his pitiful hundred feet of pitch. He looked like a giant butterfly after what I'd just seen. I called him down and hooded him. I wanted to get over to the falcons as fast as I could and see what was going on at the site of the kill.

The pigeon was dead and one of the females had control of it. She plucked it tentatively as the other two birds sat on the ground six feet away. It was impossible to tell who had actually caught the pigeon. It might have changed hands several times while I was calling Dundee down. I stayed a hundred yards away because I didn't want to frighten the falcons, and from that distance I couldn't even tell which falcon was plucking the pigeon. I suspected it was Red because she was the most aggressive. None of them seemed aggressive now. The other falcon puffed her feathers as if she might take a nap. The tiercel stood on a dirt clod and began to preen. He looked one hundred percent genuine and I took an extra moment to watch him. He was comfortable with his new status as a bona fide predator. His calmness belied the fact that he was on the ragged edge of any connection to the hack site. He didn't look wild or lethal, but he was.

The first thing I did when I got back to the house was to lock all the pigeons inside. Then I checked the hack log. Yellow had taken a full crop the night before. Red had eaten a little at five-thirty. But the tiercel, White, had not been in since the morning before. He was our bellwether and the fact that he felt independent enough to skip a meal—coupled with what I'd seen that morning—left little doubt that it was time to take in all three. I knew the tiercel was the most likely to leave. I had seen it in his posture after the pigeon kill. What I didn't know then was that the extra minutes I'd taken to watch him that morning were the last I'd ever lay eyes on him.

NOOSE CARPET. A rectangle of woven wire to which monofilament loops are tied in such a way that, when food is placed under the wire, the nooses will entangle the feet of a falcon or hawk trying to get the food.

CARRY. This term has two meanings in falconry. One is to walk with a falcon or hawk on the fist, usually as part of the training process. The second meaning refers to a vice of falcons or hawks who fly away from the falconer "carrying" quarry they have caught.

None of the falcons would be in for breakfast. Once the first falcon finished eating the kill, the other two would feast on what was left. With their full crops of fresh pigeon, we'd be lucky to see any of them by nightfall.

We had plenty of time to get the noose carpet ready but I didn't want to take any chances. I cleared the top of the hackbox of all food scraps and was securing the wire rectangle, with the thirty monofilament nooses attached, to the food board when Erney came across the yard with Little Bird hooded on his fist. He had been carrying her since sunup, exposing her to as much human contact as possible. " What's doing, Dan'l?"

"Time to cash in," I said. "Our babies have grown up." I told him what I'd seen and how I figured things. He agreed that the time had come.

"Recess is over," he said.

"You ready to start carrying a fresh one?" I asked.

Erney smiled. "Always ready for that." He stroked Little Bird's breast and she bit at him. "This sweet gal is about as tame as she gets."

We readied three sets of jesses, three bells, a half-dozen sizes of hoods. I called Pete and told him to get ready—it looked like he was going to get one of his birds back. But I didn't promise anything. There was still a lot that could go wrong.

At four o'clock the red falcon came in and sat on a telephone pole along the driveway. I sneaked out and slipped a piece of chicken under the noose carpet. If Red came in to eat she should get her toes tangled in the nooses tied to the wire. Red sat on the pole for an hour and a half. She shut her eyes one at a time and let her wings droop in the afternoon sun. At five-thirty-five Yellow came in and playfully knocked Red off the pole. They chased each other for ten minutes and disappeared over the ridge to the north.

Yellow came back at six-twenty and perched on the pole just fifteen yards from the hackbox. Red was back a few minutes later and sat on another pole. We watched Yellow from the kitchen window. I had her in the spotting scope and she was looking down at the box fifty feet below. I assumed she was eyeing the chicken under the nooses. "She's getting ready to come down," I whispered. I was concentrating on the way she was bobbing her head, so Erney's growl didn't register until he spoke.

"Pigfucker," he said. When I looked I saw that Alice was caught in the nooses by both feet.

By the time we got her untangled the nooses were a mess and the falcons were long gone. It was getting dark and there was almost no chance they'd be back before morning at the earliest. But we hustled Alice into the house and I held her until the sun was down. "So what do we do with her now?" I asked.

"Hood her up. Ship her to Saskatchewan."

"She's a wild bird. We can't hood her up."

Erney smiled as he rummaged through the papers on the kitchen table. Because my hands were full of Cooper's hawk, he held up a sheet of paper for me to read. It was a capture permit. "I thought we might need it," Erney said.

The jesses and hoods were right there, ready to be put on the peregrines. I had a foreboding feeling that we'd only need two sets at the most. "Try the tiercel hood," I said.

The next morning we were up before the sun. Alice sat hooded on the cadge on the kitchen floor, between Dundee and Little Bird. Even hooded they reacted to her the way some horses react to mules—they wanted to get as much distance between themselves and this freak as possible. The dogs were exiled to the kennel. All our energy was focused on the hackbox.

The noose carpet had been straightened out and a fresh piece of chicken slid under. The air was calm, the sky was cloudless. It was going to be a hot day; Erney and I both knew that if the falcons didn't come in that morning, they would soar. We hadn't seen the tiercel at the hackbox for forty-eight hours. That almost certainly meant he was gone. This hack, like most hacks, was speeding up to-ward the end and if the remaining falcons rose in a soar without com-ing to the hackbox, they very possibly would never come back. The next two hours would set the pattern for the coming months. It all came down to fortune. Would the falcons see a young meadowlark trying his wings for the first time before they came into the box to eat? Would a freshly flighted teal lure them to independence? It was ironic that the whole idea of a hack is to bring birds and falconers to exactly this situation. It was all or nothing: a fully hacked, perfect bird to fly, or the dream of what might have been.

Nothing moved until seven-thirty, when a pair of doves zigzagged past the window, tipped, and fluttered to the driveway to feed. It was not a good sign. They obviously felt the coast was clear. We sipped more coffee and waited as they waddled over the gravel, the male cooing to the hen. But suddenly the birds exploded from the driveway and Erney and I almost banged heads trying to see what had frightened them.

It was Yellow. She sailed lazily to the closest pole and set-tled easily, as if this was not a special morning. I had her in the spot-ting scope again and this time she was clearly hungry. She hadn't eaten the night before. Since she had no crop, apparently she had-n't eaten yet that morning, either. She bobbed her head at the chicken under the wire and launched off the pole in a mini-stoop that put her smack in the middle of the nooses. I recalled her first awkward flight and marveled at her new agility. She was physically exquisite, standing in the tangle of monofilament trying to figure out what all this nylon and wire was about. She was nearly caught and that was good, but watching her through the spotting scope I realized that I had been hoping Red would come in first. There was a chance the second bird would be frightened off when the first was caught, and my subconscious had already chosen Red as my favorite. Their appearance and powers of flight were very nearly the same, but Red had been the bird that footed me on that first day. She had dominated Alice and I thought she might be the kind of bird that could actually catch grouse in her first year. I surprised myself by admitting that what I really wanted was to consistently kill grouse with a first-year bird. I wanted to fly Red because I thought she might be the bird. But Yellow was on the carpet, and one bird was better than none.

Erney had her in the binoculars and I moved to the back door. When he saw for sure that she was caught he'd give the word and I'd sprint to the box before she pulled loose or hurt herself. It seemed to take an hour but finally Erney spoke. "She's jerking her foot. Yeah, she's caught."

I came from the house quietly but quickly. I remained hidden from her as long as I could, but once she saw that I was coming, turned, and realized she was caught, I didn't hesitate. In two bounds I was up the ladder with my left hand moving slowly over her head. She stopped trying to escape and watched the hand. Her mouth was open in fright but she was paralyzed just like any wild bird in that situation and I slipped my right hand in and secured her legs. Then I slowly lowered my left hand and tucked her slender wings into her sides.

With the wings and feet in my left hand I slipped the nooses off her feet. She was caught by two toes and I struggled with the thin nylon. Then I heard a sound that made my shoulders slump. It was the kakking of another falcon and I knew that Red was flying overhead. I didn't look. I worked as fast as I could. Once Yellow was loose, I rushed to straighten a few nooses and slipped down the ladder. As I crossed the yard I took one quick look to the sky. Empty.

It was hard to know what Red had made of the sight she'd seen as she came in. It might easily have looked like I was killing and eating her hackmate. It would take a courageous falcon indeed not to turn tail and fly for the horizon. I thought there was still a chance, but first things first.

Erney was waiting for me with a hood in his hand. It was a little small; he tried another. Perfect. Then I transferred Yellow to him and took up the bracelets for the jesses. It only took a minute to squeeze the grommets tight and slip the jesses in. I attached the swivel and belled her right leg. I was just slipping on a glove so Erney could set her up on my fist when I caught a movement out the window. "Jesus!"

Red was down on the nooses and I saw her leg jerk up as she realized she was caught. She exploded in rage. "Son of a bitch," I said as I started for the door. "Hold on, Ern."

BRACELET. Usually leather straps wrapped around the legs of a falcon or a hawk and secured with a grommet. The jesses are threaded through the grommet.

SWIVEL. The necessary metal connector between the jesses and the leash that rotates and keeps everything from twisting and endangering the trained falcon or hawk.

BELL. The act of attaching a bell to a falcon or hawk's leg.

I was back on the ladder in seconds and tried paralyzing Red with the hand-over-the-head trick. She didn't buy it. Instead of rolling back and going rigid, she leaped for the hand. When she came to the end of the noose I saw she was caught by only a talon. Another leap and she'd be free. I had to do something, so I let her foot my hand. She took it in both feet and squeezed like an eight-barreled paper punch. I caught her feet with my free hand and she leaned down and tore a chunk of skin from my knuckle.

It hurt like hell but I wasn't going to let go. She had both my hands and I had both her feet. She was still noosed and chewed on my knuckle methodically. We stared at each other, our eyes not six inches apart. She bit down on the bloody knuckle again, so I bit down on the nylon noose that held us to the hackbox. When it broke, I wrestled the falcon down the ladder as fast as I dared. On the way to the house, she bloodied two more knuckles.

Erney and I looked at each other. There wasn't a free hand between us and I was losing blood. It was hard to say if we had the birds or if the birds had us. "Put her on the cadge," I whimpered. Erney nodded. Miraculously he got her to stand upright between Dundee and Alice. When he came at Red with a hood, she snapped like a two-pound alligator. But when the hood was on she calmed down, and in five minutes she, too, stood head down and stoic on the cadge. Erney and I collapsed into chairs and started to laugh. I let my fingers bleed. "Jumping God," Erney said, "that bird's the Hell's Angel of falcons."

That's when it came to me. "Harley," I said. "We'll name her Harley." We looked at her.

"That's it," Erney said. "She's nifty as a 1959 pan head."

"She's gorgeous," I said. " And one hundred percent American made." Then we fell silent and our eyes moved to the five hooded birds. That cadge of hawks was beautiful. They were feather perfect. The bluish bloom on their backs radiated health. They sat motionless, trim packages of power and grace. Their potential seemed boundless.

Training began in earnest. The fresh birds needed to be manned. The old, intermewed birds had to be brought into good physical condition after their summer molt. Pete couldn't pick up his bird until the next day, so we treated her just like one of ours. We kept the hacked birds either on one of our fists or within a few feet for the whole first day and night. Since I was in the habit of taking naps in the afternoon, falling into the same rhythm as the dogs, the birds, and the quarry, I was better able to stay awake at night. Erney took the afternoon shift and we both carried birds in the mornings and evenings.

For the first day we were busy with the four falcons and the dogs, so we didn't pay much attention to Alice. I guess we both figured we'd haul her off and release her when we got the chance. But when Pete came and took Yellow, it left a hole in our routine. I got the bright idea of keeping Alice.

"You got to be kidding," Erney said.

I argued that I had always been fascinated by the way they flew. Training four birds was almost as easy as training three. It would be good experience.

"She's vermin," Erney said.

"Come on, don't be a speciesist. I'll bet she could catch doves." I knew that would get him since we'd failed so completely with Dundee.

"Maybe if you found a sick one," he said. "If you put some babies in a cage she'd find a way to sneak in and pull their heads off."

It took some serious negotiations but Erney finally gave in. He agreed to help man Alice and I skipped my nap to read up on manning and flying accipiters. There isn't much written about Cooper's hawks though there's a lot about their first and second cousins, the goshawk and the European sparrow hawk. We extrapo-lated from the methods used to train those famous falconry birds and came up with a plan that included intensive bareheaded carrying and a lean diet to get her flying free as soon as possible. We made a pact to keep both Harley and Alice in constant human contact for at least the next six days.

The main difference in their training at this stage was that Harley wore her hood almost constantly. Accipiters don't need to be broken to the hood (although they can be) because their flight is a sprint from the fist and they chase pretty much whatever comes up. A falcon's flight is more carefully planned; the hood makes it possible to pick and choose the best slips. In addition, falcons seem to enjoy the hood once they are used to it and accipiters are happier bare-headed. Accipiters are wilder in some ways but become very tame if extensively exposed to humans and their activities. Falcons need to be eased into this new life and hoods can help. But in both cases, from the day they are taken up the birds need to be around people without respite. They need to hear conversation, feel dogs moving around them, be taken from one perch to the other, and—most of all—come to accept the moving fist of the falconer as their home.

That meant one of us had to be awake all the time. We for-got about working on the partridge building, neglected the cattle, quit answering the telephone. We gave ourselves over to manning birds. With Alice we started out in dimly lit rooms, moving carefully, talking in low tones, stroking her breast gently. The darkened room was used with Harley, too. For several days that was the only place her hood was removed. The idea is to prove to the bird that it has nothing to fear. The results of good manning can be amazing. In a rel-atively short time a completely wild bird can become dog tame. But in some ways it's like swimming the English Channel—once you start, you need to finish. If you ease up for even a few hours it's like getting within sight of Normandy and turning back. Part of the process is waking the bird. If she once gets exhausted enough to sleep on the fist, you're nearly there. When she first rouses on the fist you know she's coming to trust you and it won't be long before she'll preen in your presence. Eventually, she'll look at you as little more than a benign creature that produces game for her.

WAKE. The training method used to keep a falcon or hawk awake and in constant contact with the falconer until it relaxes. Waking shortens the training process and greatly eases the total stress on the bird.

But the first step is getting her to eat on the fist. Food is a big deal to raptors and it definitely is the way to their hearts. Everything begins with the bird trusting the situation enough to bend over for its first bit of food from the fist.

ROUSE. To align the feathers by shaking the entire body, as a dog would dry itself.

Cooper's hawks are notorious creatures of instinct. Alice ate the first day because she couldn't help herself. She resisted for fifteen minutes in the darkened room, standing on my fist with a fresh-killed pigeon at her feet. She ignored the food and stood as if paralyzed with fright. But when I wiggled the pigeon and made a squeaking noise, she involuntarily began to foot the food. Her senses told her that the pigeon was still alive and it was more important to kill it than it was to be afraid. After piercing it a dozen times with her talons, she bent and began to eat. We increased the light in the room with every meal, and in four days she would eat readily in broad daylight.

In Harley's case, training began with slipping the hood on and off her head in low light. It's a bit tricky at first and since Erney is missing the thumb on his right hand, the initial hooding falls to me. Hooding is very important. A falcon that sits calmly and lets the hood slip over her head without a fuss is a point of pride, but more importantly she is a pleasant bird to be around. Even birds that fly well cannot be truly loved if they are hood-shy.

I like to make a game of it. I try to break a bird to the hood without it ever ducking its head or bating from the hood. I've never achieved that goal but it's worth establishing as a standard. If you go slowly enough, within an hour of the falcon's capture the braces can be loosened and tightened without any reaction. You do this by keeping the left hand—on which the falcon is standing—perfectly flat and still while you lean over and take the left brace in the fingers of your right hand. At the same time you take the right brace between your teeth and pull. This gently opens the hood. You may have to do this hundreds of times before the falcon will let you lift the hood partly off her head without a fuss. This partial unhooding and hooding needs to be done another couple of hundred times before the hood can come completely off. Then the falcon is ready for her first meal.

BRACE. One of two leather straps that open and close a hood; the act of closing a hood.

Harley was not easy to man. For two days she refused to eat. She bit me repeatedly whenever I tried to pet her. When I saw that she wasn't interested in food I had to slip the hood on to avoid a bate. On the third day, Erney cut some small pieces of chicken liver and I took Harley into the dark room along with the liver pieces and the pigeon that was intended to be her meal. Once the hood was off, I went through the usual routine of wiggling the meat. I tried the squeak trick that had worked with Alice, but Harley only stood defiant. Finally, I raised a finger to pet her. She bit as I thought she would, but this time there was a fresh piece of chicken liver on the finger. Her mandibles moved

MANDIBLE. Either segment of a bird's beak.

like lips as she tasted the liver. I offered her another piece and she took it. Then I held a tidbit on the tip of my finger and touched the pigeon at her feet. She took the liver, then began to pull at the pigeon. We were on our way.

The early hoodwork takes place in a quiet, darkened room. The light and distractions are increased over time, until the falcon will allow the hood to come off and be put back on outdoors in broad daylight with three dogs running around the house, a horse tied to the fence, and a tractor rolling past. It takes months. In fact, it is an ongoing process, and though the polish can be put on a falcon's hooding in the field, with visitors talking and gawking, the early stages are solitary work.

Some of the best parts of the late-summer training were the evenings. The days began to cool and the shadows stretched enough to allow the birds to be blocked out in the yard and have relief from the sun. The dogs were let out of the kennel and we worked with them in the yard while the birds who were most advanced in their training looked on unhooded. The Weber grill pumped pungent meat smells into the air and I let Moose run among the hooded falcons to get them used to the activity.

Every night, when the puppies were finally asleep, Little Bird and Dundee were hooded on the cadge in the kitchen, and Erney was in his cabin watching television with Alice on his fist, I sat on the deck feeling the house pulse with the day's heat. Harley was a permanent feature of my arm and once the sun was completely down and NPR's *Blues Stage* was thumping in the background, I began our nightly hooding session. Since Spud was an old hand and knew enough about this hooding thing to remain still, he was allowed to stay curled at my feet. Melvin Van Peebles serenaded us from the radio in the darkened house and the stars came on so bright it was like I was among them.

I sat on the picnic table with my feet on the bench and the yellow porch light at my back. The enormous shadow of a falconer and his bird was projected against the lone cottonwood in the yard. Those nights I thought about Kris. I wondered what it was really like, tweaking the chemistry of a person at death's door. I thought about the hunting season that would start very soon. Harley would not be ready for another week but I had a good feeling about her. She had been a tough nut to crack but three-quarters of the way through her manning she had made a great reversal and begun to excel in training the way she had at hack. I could barely contain my expectations for her. Sharp-tailed grouse had begun appearing when I worked the dogs, and, although our first-year birds were usually used mostly for ducks, I had a feeling about Harley.

Spud was back in the groove, running with only an intermittent limp right to where the birds were and pointing like a million. Melville was slow but dependable, always checking back to be sure I was coming, enjoying every minute. I'd had some trouble with Moose. For all her seeming boldness, flushing birds frightened her. I had undertaken a bird encouragement course. Every day I took a chicken out with us, and let it go in full sight of her. This was breaking a dog of chicken chasing—only in reverse. I squealed with excitement and chased the chicken around madly. Moose was skeptical, but when I got down on all fours, sniffed the grass, barked, and pounced on the confused chicken, she began to get the idea. She was going to be all right.

I was tired of the training, the manning, the hooding. I was ready for the season and had already picked the pond where we'd start Little Bird on ducks. We were about to begin hunting. But the training would go on. It never ends. I held Harley up and looked her over. She was a beautiful bird, like the passage peregrines we used to trap on southern beaches. She wasn't big, coming to the lure at thirty ounces. But her heart seemed big and courage is the main element of good flights. I slipped the hood off and glanced into her eyes. They were as black and shiny as the head of a salmon fly. If I hooded her just right, nothing moved but the nictitating membrane, coming up from the well of those eyes. She sat calmly and I looked out to the shadow falconer and his bird against the cottonwood. The hood came off again and was returned. Then off very slowly. And on again.

Off. And I wondered what Kris was doing at that very moment. On, off. Tighten the braces. I stroked Harley's chest. Loosen the braces. On, off, on. Spud resettled himself and I took the hood off so Harley could see him move. She paid no attention. On again.

Off again. On. A slight breeze tattled in the cottonwood and our image blurred. Time stretched out. The hood went on. The hood came off. On. Off. Again. Again. Slowly. Gently, without touching the beak. Again and one eye went shut. Eighty-seven. Eighty-eight. Both eyes shut. Eighty-nine. Again. Again. Even as she slept.

Reclaiming the intermewed birds, Dundee and Little Bird, was mostly a matter of jogging their memories. They knew what they were supposed to do; once they got hungry they could be released and they would return to a lure garnished with meat. After that, all they needed was to fly. A couple of weeks on the wing and they would be ready to hunt.

Alice and Harley were another matter. They needed to learn to come when called and to be comfortable eating on the ground in front of us. Accipiters are taught primarily to fly to the fist, while falcons are more comfortable coming to the lure. We usually train our falcons to come to the fist too, but seldom ask them to do it in the field. This makes them easier to pick up from the blocks, and repeated jumping to the fist can help keep them in shape during periods of bad weather. For both birds the lesson began the same way.

At feeding time the birds were brought into the darkened room again. But this time they were put on a screen perch. The food, on my fist, was held out in front of them so that they had to jump to get it. Usually birds ignore the food once they see they have to jump to it, and they take some coaxing. Again, Alice was easy to trick. I let a pigeon wing hang loose from my fist and flapped it suddenly. She couldn't resist and was on the fist footing and mantling before she knew what she was doing. She looked as surprised as I was—embarrassed even—at her own avarice.

Harley needed to be sweet-talked. She stood on the perch and glared at the food. If I wiggled it, she would stretch her neck out and try to pull it to her. But I held tight and she would not jump. On the second day she tried to make a long step and nearly fell off the perch. Finally, I lay my forearm on the perch in front of her and wiggled the meat. She stepped onto my arm and walked out to her meal. It took three days to get her actually to jump to the fist. Once she began, though, I stood four feet away and she flew readily.

The first day that we moved outside, both birds flew to the fist several times. Soon they wanted to fly farther than the leash would allow, so we began using a creance. By the end of the week Alice would fly from Erney to me and back at a distance of fifty feet.

Once Harley was coming fifteen feet from the block to the fist on the creance, we introduced her to the lure. Falcons love the lure. They much prefer to eat on that leather disk thrown on the ground than on the fist. Harley made the switch with no trouble. Soon she was coming to the lure too far for the creance to be anything but a hindrance. One day I intended to call her off a fence post in front of the house but she left on her own before I had even swung the lure. She actually came over and waited for me to get the lure out of the bag. She would have made a circle if the creance hadn't gotten tangled. When the creance starts to be a pain in the neck, it's time to fly the falcon free.

LEASH. Usually a leather strap about three feet in length and one half inch wide with a "button" on the end. This allows the swivel to turn while the other end of the leash is tied to the perch.

CREANCE. A long, strong string used to ensure that a falcon or hawk will not fly away in the initial stages of training.

CALL OFF. To call a hawk to the fist or a falcon to the lure for food.

Erney and I had already decided that we would not bother putting radio telemetry on Alice. Coops don't fly nearly as far as falcons and besides, she had never shown any signs of leaving us. We simply turned Alice loose, and she didn't seem to notice that she was free. She continued to fly back and forth from Erney's fist to mine for tidbits. But Harley was a different story. As with the other falcons, Erney and I agreed that she should never be turned loose without telemetry. Transmitters are not foolproof by a long shot but they can be a godsend if a falcon is out of sight—down on game or drifted away.

The old batteries in both the receiver and the transmitter were replaced. A leather bewit was cut to hold the tiny transmitter to Harley's leg. While she was hooded we made the transmitter fast and checked to make sure it was working. The reassuring beep was loud and clear. I walked out in front of the house, unhooded Harley, and let her jump to the fence post she was used to. Everything was just as it had been the day before except now she was free. Now she could fly to China if she wanted.

But she didn't. She jumped off the post and came to me again before I produced the lure. She made a circle and then a second circle. When I tossed the lure out, she dived for it as if she'd been doing this all her life. She settled in to eat without even considering me. Now that I had a way to get her back, we could move on to the real thing. We could begin to work on a hunting strategy. I knelt beside her as she took her meal from the lure. The first stage of training was over. Now all she needed was air time, then game. Lots of game.

On the fourth of September, the falconry season began. Because it takes so long to get a falcon flying well, because the impact on game is negligible, and because it would be a mistake to force falconers into the field when gun hunters are everywhere, the season is seven months long. I used to fly birds most of that time, but as I got older, South Dakota's below-zero winters convinced me that the time to hawk is September, October, and November. I'm still weak enough to keep hawking after the first of the year if conditions are good and I have an excellent game hawk gracing my mews. But a concentrated effort during those first three months of the season is better than a partial effort over the long haul. That is part of what this equinox autumn was about. I felt a pressing need to focus my life the way I focused my falconry, to get things tied up and figured out before the cold dark winter set in.

The ducks, which are a big part of our falconry, are usually gone by the second week in November. If the falcons are ready to go in the beginning of September—and you have set the time aside—three months is plenty. This year we were ready. I had only the commitment to go woodcock hunting and, as always, that wasn't until the second week in October. Other than that, it was all falconry until the temperature dipped out of sight.

By the first week in September, after an initial period where I felt uneasy leaving Erney alone with Alice, they had seemed to bond. Erney still cursed her, but he'd gone sweet on her and she was on his fist constantly. She was flying back and forth between us for food at distances of up to a hundred yards. Harley had tamed down and as soon as she figured out that the lure swung around my head meant dinner, she entered into a steep learning curve. She was flying free and beginning to make ascending circles waiting for me to produce the lure. This was the first step in making a game hawk; she had achieved it in only two weeks.

There was still no change in Dundee. His flying could take the breath away from the casual observer but in truth he was a pansy and only flying for fun. A movie production crew called to ask if I'd fly a falcon for a film. They needed a bird mounting into a sunset. I knew it would take many tries to get it right and that no real game hawk would tolerate being put up and taken down at the whim of a Hollywood director. I've had some experience with movie people, and some aren't too well grounded in reality. I didn't want to take time out to fool with a movie, but finally they cajoled—and bribed—me into it.

An academic friend from Iowa named John was visiting that day and I dragged him along to assist. I flew Dundee on the eastern edge of the Black Hills, and, as I'd suspected, they wanted him to go up time and again. "Let's try it once more," the mirror-sunglassed director would shout from his enclave of vehicles, cameras, and assistants. Sometimes he'd send his blond-haired gofer out to explain what he wanted.

I had briefly removed Dundee's hood to the astonished gasps of the crowd gathered around the director. There were actually a couple of cheers when I cast him off. It was as if this were Kitty Hawk, North Carolina, and I was Orville Wright. Five minutes later, at the signal of the blond assistant, who was particularly awed by the bird and the sunset and the miles of grass surrounding us, I called Dundee down to the lure. I hooded him up without feeding because I knew they'd want him to do it again. The assistant ran out to where I stood. "Wow," he said, "that was definitely awesome." He was a big, beautiful man about thirty—one of those "too good-looking to be real" guys—and even though he was enamored with Dundee, he didn't come too close. "Those talons are sharp as knives, huh?"

"Sharper," John said. "Like scalpels." This surprised me. John isn't much of a talker, but apparently he found these movie people even more absurd than the university people he worked with. I suppose he couldn't resist. "If you don't know what you're doing," he said slowly, "they can slash you to ribbons in an instant."

I had to join the fun. "You can't believe the power," I said and looked down at Dundee, all eighteen ounces of him. I squinted and shook my head grimly as if it took courage just to hold him.

"This is so out-of-sight," Blondie said. It took him a moment to remember why he'd run out to us. "Sydney wants him a little farther to the left, so we can get the majesty of his flight against that mountain." He pointed to one of the hills to the west.

"I'll do my best," I said.

For the first few flights Dundee didn't seem to mind not being fed. He came down to the lure, chipped at me, jumped onto my fist, and leaned forward to get his hood on. But as the sun slid closer to the hills and Dundee's dinnertime drew nearer, we both got impatient. A real game hawk would have been gone by now. It was against all falconry principles to let a falcon go and not do your best at least to give him something to chase. Only a completely tame bird would put up with this sort of nonsense but even Dundee was capable of flying away out of boredom. I did have a homing pigeon in my pocket, one that Dundee could never catch, so I could give him the reward of a chase and the pigeon would simply fly home. On the seventh take I told Blondie, who was nearly worn out from running the fifty yards back and forth to give us direction for Sydney's latest aesthetic inspiration, that this was the last time.

I put Dundee up and I left him there for as long as I dared. I really did hope Sydney got what he wanted but Dundee needed a little something too. I smiled at John. "Watch this," I said, and flipped out the pigeon.

It's hard to know what came over Dundee. It was as if he had heard John and me teasing the assistant. From his pitiful pitch of a hundred and fifty feet he seemed to turn inside out. He didn't fold his wings. He pumped all the way down and hit the pigeon with a crack that sent the pigeon tumbling end over end right into the middle of the camera crew. Trained peregrine falcons almost never catch good pigeons, but when they do, they almost always pick awkward times. This was as awkward as it gets.

When John and I got there, people were scattered. Chairs were upset, cameras tipped over. Two women were crying. Sydney's sunglasses were askew at the end of his nose and Blondie was telling people to stand back. "He can tear you to shreds in an instant," he shouted.

Dundee had the pigeon's head off and was merrily plucking its breast in anticipation of a fantastic dinner. This was what I most feared about flying a falcon for a movie in the first place—bringing that question of not being grounded in reality to a head. This crowd had long since sacrificed any ability they might have had to understand my reality, let alone Dundee's. I felt that an explanation of the undeniable but neutral role of death and predation in all life would not be worth the effort.

MAKE IN. To approach a trained bird of prey on its kill.

I kept my mouth shut and made in to Dundee. I knelt on the ground and busied myself with jesses and swivel, trying to think what I would say when I stood up. But I didn't have to worry. Blondie spoke his line as if it were scripted and John responded with a calmness that put everyone's mind at ease.

"Is that a real pigeon?" Blondie asked.

"No," John answered. His pause would have turned Jack Benny green with envy. "But he plays one on TV."

There are probably twenty-five duck ponds within five miles of the ranch and we've named most of them: Back Pasture Pond, Middle Pond, Berger's, The Hyway Pond, Steve's Corner Pond,

Chet's Lower Pond. For about eight weeks each year, before the ponds freeze solid, we have good duck hawking. In productive years it's excellent. Because that summer had been wet there were ducks everywhere. We could be choosy. If we had a hotshot, experienced bird, one who was hard from a month of continuous hawking, we might try to find a pond with big, tough mallards. To get the best flight out of her, we might locate a pond with an approach that, if the falcon was going to have a chance, forced her to wait on upwind. With a young bird who needed an easy duck, we might have taken her to a pond with gadwalls and a dam that would allow us to flush the ducks at just the right moment.

I wanted the easiest slip we could find for Little Bird. Although she'd killed lots of release partridge and quite a few wild ones, she had never killed a duck. Erney had tried her a couple of times her first year and concluded that she just didn't like them. It does happen that some birds simply don't like ducks, but I had always contended they could all learn to like them. It had been a debate between Erney and me. Since Little Bird was a partridge specialist, though, I never felt the urge to prove my theory. This season she had already made a couple of partridge kills from a nice pitch over Spud and Melville's points, and Erney lobbied to forget about ducks. But this was my equinox autumn and getting Little Bird to kill ducks was one of the things on my list.

I put the big day off until I found a group of teal on a tiny piece of water we call the Little Corner Pond. Teal can be nearly useless as falcon quarry. They are not the most confident flyers and often won't leave the water with a falcon in the air. They are the pheasant of the duck world and, like pheasants, will commit an amazing array of cowardly acts to avoid having to put their powers of flight to the ultimate test. But also like pheasants, in the right situation they can be quarry par excellence.

The Corner Pond was the right situation. A berm of dirt concealed the flushers until they were right up on the ducks. Once the ducks got flying there was no place for them to hide, just two miles of short grass. We had all the dogs and all the birds in the pickup. Everyone was getting into the routine now that the season was upon us. We planned to take the setters to a grouse field for some work, then the new birds to the training grounds. But first we'd try Little Bird.

When Erney saw the setup, he scoffed. "You call this a slip? It's hardly fair."

It was a little embarrassing. "It's her first duck," I said.

"She hates ducks. She won't even take one with a slip this easy."

"She'll take one."

"She just doesn't like ducks," Erney said. He had Alice on his fist and slid carefully from the pickup seat. I would be flying Little Bird and flushing the teal with Moose along for the drill. Erney, being unable to do much walking, was there as an observer. His main function was to document this historic event.

Wind is a tricky thing in falconry. You have to keep in mind that if it's blowing more than a few miles per hour, the quarry must take off into it. The falcon is most successful when she stoops with the wind at her back. But the quarry knows that

MAKE. To successfully en-
courage a falcon to kill.

better than you and does everything it can to flush when the falcon is downwind and will almost never give her a better shot than a crosswind stoop. All this wind-chess makes the good flights interesting. But wind is always a complicating factor. When you're trying to make a hawk, it's best to have none. As I walked toward the pond, with Moosey leaping to the height of my shoulder in kind of a floating heel, I was pleased to feel nothing but warm afternoon sun on my face. This was a lowlife slip—small pond, young ducks, approaching from behind a dirt bank, and no wind—though it was just what Little Bird needed to get her interested in ducks.

I made Moosey hup and unhooded Little Bird when we were a hundred and fifty yards from the pond. By this time Little Bird's mind, if not her body, was back to hunting trim. She stood on the fist and let her feathers fluff. She squinted, and roused leisurely.

HUP. Traditional command used for hunting dogs; to lie down.

Then she spread her wings and hopped into the air. Little Bird's strongest characteristic is that she almost always goes up very high. Coming down is where she has her problem. I knew that if she was ever going to stoop at a duck she'd have to be hungry. For the occasion I had trimmed her weight to an ounce under her partridge flying weight. My hope was that she wouldn't mess around.

I'm sure Little Bird thought Moose was along to flush a partridge for her. She went up in her signature way, lining out for a half mile at a forty-five-degree angle, making a slow turn and climbing all the way back. It's not the best way for a falcon to gain her pitch—it gives the quarry a chance to flush when she is far off—but the main thing is getting up high, and that she did well. By the time Moose and I had made it to the dirt bank, Little Bird was just a speck above us. I looked back at Erney with the binoculars. He was leaning against the pickup with Alice on his fist and squinting upward. I knew he was thinking that because Little Bird had refused those ducks several years ago, she'd refuse them

REFUSE. To pass up the opportunity to chase game.

now. As I waited for her to make a turn so the pond would be right in front of her, I had a moment of doubt.

But this was the best chance Little Bird would ever have. It was now or never. I walked around the bank and sent Moose ahead with the flick of my hand.

She charged the water and would probably have leaped in if the teal had stayed. But the ducks rose off as soon as they saw us. They either didn't see Little Bird up there or they didn't have much fear of her. It's not unheard of, but it's rare that game lose track of a falcon in the air above. The way they took off more likely meant that they weren't really afraid of Little Bird. That notion made my heart sink. Wild birds seem to know when a falcon is a threat; when a falcon is not serious they pay no attention to it. That's exactly what looked to be happening here.

I found Little Bird in the sky. She was very high and could have caught the teal easily if she would only try. I yelled, hoping that might excite her. She flew in the same direction as the teal but far above them, showing no sign of starting a stoop. They were all heading toward the gravel road where the pickup was parked and I knew Erney would be able to see the teal easily by then. But Little Bird stayed high. It was as if she were just watching them, a classic refusal tactic. I gritted my teeth and kicked the dirt.

But then she folded. She didn't flap a wing, she just came over in an arch to vertical and plummeted. The problem was that the teal were a quarter of a mile in front of her now, almost to the road. I didn't know what she was doing until I got her in the binoculars and saw her level out over the ground. She must have been going two hundred miles per hour when she passed through the flock of ducks.

I don't think she hit one, but they all decided the air was no place to be and crashed into grazed grass on the other side of the road. In the binoculars, teal bounced like popcorn. Little Bird must not have been able to stand it. She pitched up, rolled over, and pinned one to the prairie. From the pickup I heard a distant cheer. Erney must have thought I couldn't see what was happening because he waved his hat, our signal for a kill. I turned the binoculars on him and saw a big smile on his face as he and Alice hobbled down the road toward Little Bird.

It was not the most determined flight we'd ever seen, but she'd caught a duck and that was a start. Erney, even though he'd cheered, grumbled about how it was probably just luck. I was chuckling as we drove up our driveway toward where we intended to work the setters and fly the new birds. But we both fell silent when a flock of eight sharptails sailed across the road in front of us. I pulled to a stop in the middle of the driveway and the birds settled into the stubble to the right and two hundred yards out. Erney and I automatically marked the spot, then turned and looked at each other. We were within sight of the house. It was a field Harley had flown over ever since she could fly. They were young, dumb grouse. Melville and Spud were in the back. It was cooling toward evening and the wind was dead calm.

"We shouldn't do this," I said.

"Good slip," Erney said.

We looked back out to be sure we knew where the grouse were.

"We always start them on ducks," I said.

"What could it hurt?"

"Things could get crazy. She doesn't know what we're doing. We could lose her."

"Lose her? She was hacked here."

"We'd never get them pointed. They're air-washed. The dogs would bump them."

"If they don't point them, don't fly her."

AIR-WASHED. The loss of scent that game birds undergo by flying. Such birds are difficult for dogs to scent immediately after the flight.

Because so much can go wrong, the great falconers are not determined so much by their ability to fly their birds as by their ability to say no. I looked back at Erney. "We shouldn't do this," I said.

"I know," he said. "But you can't stand it."

He was right. We let Melville and Spud out and walked into the shin-high stubble. Harley was on my fist and Alice was on Erney's. Old Spud knew this game and loved it. Now his limp was gone. He moved without any sign of pain and I had to keep growling at him to heel. We stopped ten yards out and all four of us—Erney, Melville, Spud, and I—looked out to the area where the grouse had landed. Thick stubble is an excellent place to fly grouse. This was tall enough for them to hold but not thick enough to make them impossible to catch if they were knocked to the ground. The tricky part would be locating them exactly. Harley had only been flown free half a dozen times. She wasn't going to wait on long, and to have any chance the grouse would have to be flushed at exactly the right moment. That meant we needed a point. The grouse were a little close to the fence that ran along the end of the field but if we could get a point it might be a great slip.

It's hard to describe the tension of a flight at grouse with a new bird. It's very different from duck hawking because the falconer has much less control of the situation, grouse are more wily than ducks, they are more confident fliers, tougher, and are capable of leaving a tentative falcon in their contrail. They will use fences or high wires as protection from stoops; more than a few naive falcons have had the tables turned on them and ended up dissected by power lines.

Erney and I stood surveying our position with some trepidation. Melville and Spud sat beside us and Spud whined, excited to the edge of control. I like to wait ten minutes for grouse to put down some scent but that day I couldn't stand it. Without taking my eyes off the spot, I whispered, "All right." There was the sound of charging dog and we watched Spud, suddenly as lively as a puppy, begin to work the stubble in front of us. Even at ten years old he was a classy devil, high head, merry tail. It was a joy to watch him work that big field where his particular style could be used to full advantage.

He ran seventy yards to the left, then cut back in front of us. When he got seventy yards to our right he turned like I'd jerked his collar. He worked back across, fifty feet farther into the field. I didn't have to say a word. He kept quartering farther and farther away. Erney and I squinted and concentrated, searching for any hesitation that might indicate birds. Then it dawned on me. "Where's Melville?" Erney and I looked at each other.

Then our eyes slid down to find Melville, sitting between us, squinting and concentrating on Spud with the same expression on his face that we had had. If he could've spoken he'd have said something like, "Isn't Spud amazing? I love to watch a good dog run."

Erney laughed and I booted Melville. "Get out there," I said. He sprang forward and galloped after Spud as if he had played a great trick on us.

Spud was still working his ground well but had already passed the place I would have bet the grouse to be. Erney must have had it figured the same way. "Did he miss them?"

Just then, Spud slammed to a stop like he'd hit a glass wall. His tail came up in a sickle arch. "Nope," I said as I reached to strike the braces of Harley's hood.

Melville was still a hundred yards behind, but when he saw Spud pointing he honored as if the birds were just under his nose. I took Harley's hood off and she looked out to Spud's tight, high-headed point and Melville's long flowing back. She knew the dogs well but she'd never seen them on point before. An old bird knows all about dogs on point. The good ones take to the air immediately and climb for a place high above and upwind of the dog's nose. They know exactly what the dogs are doing and they wait in position until the birds are flushed. That behavior is mostly a conditioned response, of course, but there is also a kind of predatory communication between dogs and falcons. Harley seemed to sense what was happening and pushed off without rousing. As soon as she was in the air I started forward. Erney stayed behind because of his leg and because Alice was still unhooded and on his fist. We didn't want her bating and Harley mistaking her for the quarry.

Since the air was calm I didn't bother trying to swing around the dogs to force the grouse downwind. I walked first to Melville, stroked him, and told him he was a good boy, then walked on to Spud and stood twenty feet behind him while Harley gained some altitude. I reminded Spud that he needed to stay put. "Whoa," I whispered. "Easy."

Harley didn't know what we were doing but she circled and started up. When she was a couple hundred feet up I decided I'd better not get greedy. Two hundred feet is not usually high enough to catch grouse, but this was an introduction and I was confident that she was not

WHOA. Traditional command used for hunting dogs; to stop.

going to catch one anyway. I just wanted her to see them, hear their whirr-glide, whirr-glide, and stoop hard. If she'd just do that much, and we got her back, I'd be tickled. So when she made her next circle I stepped up beside Spud. I knelt and waited while her back was turned. When she was facing the right direction, I stood up again and moved forward as she came overhead.

Spud has never been completely broke and as I moved he leaped past me like a bobcat. Three grouse sprang from the stubble. Although I had figured Harley would go for them because all falcons love grouse, her intensity surprised me. By the time I looked up she had flipped and was driving double-time toward the last grouse to come up. Then she made a young bird mistake. She stooped to where the grouse was. With ducks this works fine, but grouse are too fast on the flush and a falcon needs to anticipate where they are going to be. I smiled, expecting that her error had finished her. There is not much room for mistakes with grouse—one shot per grouse is usually all a falcon gets. But Harley was not done. Her stoop flattened out behind the grouse and she stayed right on it. Even to keep up with a grouse once the pitch is gone is rare, yet Harley was actually pressing it by the time they neared the edge of the field. Once the falcon was out of the airspace above, the rest of the flock came up around me but I didn't let myself be distracted. I couldn't believe Harley was staying with the grouse. I jogged toward the flight in an attempt to keep them in sight as they approached the berm of the driveway. What I didn't want was for Harley to follow the grouse for a mile and then get blown away and find herself alone and hungry and out of my sight—a combination for disaster.

BROKE. Description of a completely trained pointing dog. A broke dog does not chase game but stands steady when birds are flushed and shot.

I didn't have to worry. Harley, though still ten feet behind the grouse, had somehow gotten above it. This was the maneuver of an experienced falcon and it was clear that the grouse was concerned. It was also clear that it was a young grouse. An old grouse would simply have accelerated at a forty-five-degree angle and blown Harley's doors off. But she had this grouse rattled, and it was looking for a place to hide. If it landed on the ground it would be safe. It would evade Harley's pass, then hide in the grass until she settled in to look for it. At the perfect time the grouse would jump up and be a hundred yards away by the time Harley beat herself out of the grass and into the air again. But there was a determination in Harley's wing beat that was like nothing I'd ever seen in a young bird. She thought she was going to catch this grouse and she had the grouse believing it too.

They were going top speed, too fast to be in control. I had a good view of them and expected them to disappear over the driveway. But something strange happened. The grouse suddenly disappeared. One instant it was there, flying as hard as it could, the next it was gone and Harley was shooting upward. She hung at the zenith of her pitch-up and everything slowed to half speed. She studied the ground over her shoulder, then flipped. Her wing beat went back to double-time and she stooped vertically and hard, right into the ground.

It took an instant to register, but as I ran toward her I realized exactly what had happened. The grouse had hit the fence that ran along the driveway. It had been pressured and perhaps was looking back when the top strand of barbed wire clotheslined it out of the air. It was impossible to gauge the damage to the grouse but I expected it to jump up and fly off any second. It could also have been hurt or stunned long enough for Harley to get a grip on it.

That would be a lousy way to catch a grouse, but an excellent way to enter a falcon. Falcons don't care so much about the aesthetics of the sport. A kill is a kill. The experience of catching the first grouse it saw could be indelible for a falcon. More than half of grouse hawking is a mind game. As with any athlete, whatever a falcon believes about its abilities becomes a self-fulfilling prophecy. Because they so often fail in the early going, most falcons come to think they can't catch grouse and so quit trying hard. But a few always believe they can catch any grouse that flies, so they do. It's a hard quality to develop without an early break.

> ENTER. To introduce a falcon or hawk to its intended quarry.

I held my breath as I approached where the birds had disappeared. The dogs were coming up behind me and I whoaed them and made them hup. I didn't want them scaring Harley, flushing the uninjured grouse, or catching it if it was hurt. I moved very slowly, listening for the bell, talking gently so Harley would know it was me. Erney had walked down the driveway and now stood on that higher ground scanning the same area. We didn't talk. We both knew what had happened and we both knew that if we found Harley on a grouse it meant luck had smiled on us. We also knew that Harley was most likely standing somewhere in the grass in front of us, wondering where the grouse had gone.

I heard the flutter of wings the instant Erney spoke. "There she is." He pointed ten feet in front of me. I couldn't see her but I heard the wings again. This time it was familiar. It was the death rattle of a grouse. When I took another step Harley raised her head out of the grass. Her eyes sparkled and her beak was dripping blood.

We let her eat all she wanted. I sat in the grass beside her and the dogs crawled up to get their petting. The sun was heading in for the night and I couldn't have been happier. We were less than a quarter of a mile from the house. Since Harley was taking her time, I told Erney to drive on in and get the Weber fired up.

Harley stood on her grouse and I stroked her while she ate. She let me tear tidbits from the grouse breast and she ate them from my hand. Harley had decapitated the grouse. That was her part of the ritual. I surreptitiously slipped the head away. Out of her sight, I dug a hole in the soft earth with my pocket knife and dropped in the grouse head. I pushed the dirt in on top and held my hands tight over the fresh soil. I closed my eyes for a few seconds—my part complete—then turned back to Harley. Though I'd been in that position many times, something stirred inside me. "You've got what it takes," I told her. I rubbed Melville's ears as he sidled in and tried to ease a piece of grouse from Harley. She reached out and bit him lightly on the nose. He looked at me like an embarrassed kid. "You'll get your share," I said. I rubbed Spud's ears, too. He seemed old again. "You too, Spud. We'll all get our share. But Harley eats first."

My share included half a teal and half a partially eaten grouse. Melville and Spud got the livers and hearts. They ate theirs raw but Erney and I slow-roasted ours over a hardwood fire. We pulled out a couple of extra partridge from the freezer and basted all the birds with olive oil. Erney would have been happy with just the meat but I have my principles. Eating should not be discriminatory. The term "vegetarian" is only a socially accepted description of a picky eater, and pure carnivores are not much better. I insisted on throwing a few potatoes and peppers on the grill.

The roasting took a full hour. As the smells matured, Erney and I took our beers out to our little garden for a standing salad. We have a rule that there is no canning or freezing of vegetables at the ranch. Our garden is strictly for grazing. We stood among the rows and crunched on string beans and carrots. We sipped beer in the cooling evening and watched the sun set. I ate a radish and a very ripe strawberry. Erney had a kohlrabi. We relived the flights. Erney was still extremely skeptical about Little Bird as a duck hawk. He insisted that she was wed to partridge and thought the fact that she actually caught a duck only meant that it was a very easy duck. I maintained

WED. To be intent on a certain quarry to the exclusion of all other quarry.

that now that she knew ducks were a lot like partridge, she was made. We did agree that the next weeks would tell the story. By the time I left to join Kris for my ten days in the Northeast, we should know a lot more. We picked a handful of snap peas for the walk back to the house.

It was going to be a full two weeks. One of our jobs would be to find a niche for Alice. We'd been trying to get her to chase the rabbits around the yard, but she showed little interest. We wondered if she was going to make it. Dundee had been turned into pretty much a pet. But Little Bird and Harley should keep us busy. There were a million local ducks that year and the northern ones were beginning to move in. We agreed that Harley should be focused on them for experience and only flown at grouse when the slip was an excellent one.

As we cut into the roasted birds, Erney and I were both doing our best not to put into words our high hopes for Harley as a grouse hawk. Harley had been a good prospect from the beginning and that day's flight was a lucky stroke, but we didn't want to jinx her future by talking about it. We concentrated on the meat. It was smoky, crisp on the outside where the olive oil had browned into a crust and, under that, a uniform pink to the bone. We drank more beer and washed everything down with a snifter of port.

Moose and Melville went to sleep early, but Spud stayed out on the deck with me long after Erney had gone back to his cabin. He lay with his head against my foot. I leaned down and rubbed his ear and he didn't move except for two light tail thumps. I noticed his graying muzzle. He'd done his job so well that day that we'd taken him for granted. I couldn't help thinking that he knew he wasn't going to make the woodcock trip that year. It would be the first road trip he'd miss since he was a pup. But it was a tough one for any dog, six hard days of hunting in wet weather with a two-day ride in a dog box at each end. Even at ten years old, with a bad leg, he had too much heart to do anything but give one hundred percent. Kris and I had agreed that he might hurt himself, and if he did, we'd never forgive ourselves. He and Moosey could help Erney find birds for the falcons. Melville was our brush dog, anyway.

As if my thoughts had commanded him, Melville came to the doorway and scratched to come out with us. Since I didn't want to move my foot and disturb Spud, I leaned way back and slid the door open. Mel yawned as he came onto the deck, stopped beside me long enough to accept a pet, then lay down with his head over Spud's back. Without Moose leaping in Mel's wake, Spud was content to have him near. In fact, they were great hunting buddies. I would miss finding them both stacked up on point in a side hill of golden poplars.

In the weeks leading up to the woodcock hunt, we were all busy indeed. Harley took to ducks the way we figured she would, and after her fourth gadwall we moved up to mallards on bigger ponds. She took them, too, but none of her duck flights was spectacular. She did not go up high; she simply caught the ducks when they made a break for it. We didn't look for grouse, but on a couple of occasions we saw slips that were too good to pass up. Then the wing beat of the grouse seemed to excite her. She flew with much more flair and force, but didn't catch one. We didn't want to discourage her and decided to keep building her confidence with ducks. I planned to put in a few serious days of grouse hawking just before I left for New Brunswick.

Little Bird caught a few more ducks but it was tough. True to Erney's predictions, she flew hard only when she wanted to, and we couldn't figure out exactly what made her really want to. It did become clear that she flew harder when Erney stayed at home. Over the years she had bonded with Erney, who did most of the feeding during the molting season. The first part of the molting season is also the breeding season and she had laid an egg that spring. We theorized that she wanted Erney to be the father of that egg and, as would good fathers in most species, she expected him to provide for it and her. When Erney was near the duck pond, she would chase the ducks, but I believe she expected him to catch them and feed them to her. Needless to say, that was not what we were interested in. She flew ducks for me and flew release partridge over Spud and Mel's points like she always did, very high and very successfully. I came to the end of that first part of the season with mixed feelings about her and determined to make her my focus when I returned and the northern ducks came down in force.

Meanwhile, Erney and I were doing everything we could think of to get Alice catching rabbits. Erney had carried her almost constantly for three weeks and she was very tame. She would chase rabbits but didn't want to close with them, so we tried lowering her weight. She came into the mystic physical and mental state of yarak—a condition of accipiters in which their entire bearing changes and every fiber is focused on game. But even that didn't seem to make much difference, and neither Erney nor I had the stomach to lower her more. When we walked her, as we often did before and after training sessions, she would bate and hit the end of her leash if a small bird came up at our feet but would act like she didn't see them if they started twenty feet away. There were only a few days left before Melville and I went out to meet Kris when an idea struck me.

YARAK. A state of high physical and mental readiness in hawks that stimulates them to high performance when hunting.

The next morning Erney and I were in the pickup cruising the wheat stubble. There are a few places near the ranch where doves gather at that time of year. I'd tried them a hundred times with Dundee but all he did was fly around and force them to sit tight. He looked like a real falcon to them and their evolution taught them that they were safest hiding on the ground. When I walked around with Dundee in the air they would wait until the last possible moment to flush. They were, of course, perfectly safe with Dundee, but I reasoned that it might be a different story with Alice. The trick was to get them to come up at my feet and give Alice the close slip she seemed to like.

Doves don't recognize a bird on a falconer's fist. They only see the falconer. Walking around with Alice on the fist would only spook the doves at great distances, so we flew Dundee first. When we spotted some doves, we put Dundee up, and that froze them to the ground. Dundee loved this and zoomed around looking ferocious. When he had convinced the doves that their best chance was to hold fast, I swung the lure and Dundee screamed back as if his life depended on it. Erney popped Dundee's hood on while I carried Alice out to where the doves cowered. They were thinking that the terrible peregrine falcon might still be within striking distance. The first dove that got up flushed from under my right foot and Alice had it before it went two yards. She hit it hard enough that Erney heard the collision back at the truck.

It happened so fast that my breath actually caught. It looked so simple! Had the dove been sick? But when I made in to Alice and saw the big, healthy, mature dove that she mantled over, it came clear to me what is meant when people describe Cooper's hawks as sprinters. Alice was programmed for flights just like this. "Holy moly," Erney said.

He was standing over my shoulder as I eased my gloved hand under Alice and raised her and her dove off the ground. Her wings were spread to hide and protect her kill from the greedy eyes of other predators. The feathers on the top of her head were flared into a crest and her eyes were wild. This was no noble falcon. Alice looked like something out of a Spielberg movie. "Holy moly," Erney said again. "If she weighed four pounds, cattle wouldn't be safe."

You'd think that the most important element for good grouse hawking would be lots of grouse. A cloud of sharptails makes your heart race and it does make for good hawking. But the key to successful hawking is good ground. It should be reasonably flat so the grouse aren't always popping over the next hill and disappearing. It should be wide open, with only a few bushes in the draws. The grass should be eight to sixteen inches high—tall enough that birds feel safe sitting for a point but short enough to make bailing out in front of an oncoming stoop a bad evasive maneuver. There should be grouse in small groups scattered throughout, and miles to the nearest real trees. It should be isolated because solitude is a big part of good falconry.

I have a special place like that. It's twenty-two hundred acres of land twenty miles from our house in Rapid City, an hour's drive from the ranch. Even though my part of South Dakota is not famous for its grouse, I have never failed to find at least one slip there.

It is big country that makes the grouse tough and I almost never bother taking a bird there until she is killing ducks with almost no effort. That's usually Thanksgiving of her first year, and even then the results are often poor. For trained peregrine falcons, sharp-tailed grouse are difficult to the point of the ridiculous. To kill even one in good style is an accomplishment. But when it happens, especially in November, December, and January, when the grouse are experienced and hard, it's sublime.

Only because Harley had been something of a prodigy did I bother to take her to my special place. It was the second week in October, three days before Melville and I were to catch a plane for Boston, and the air was crisp and laced with autumn. I must have felt something different in that air because I left all birds and dogs at the ranch except Harley and Spud. I was nervous about losing Harley and tried to think of everything. I broke with personal tradition and put a live lure pigeon in my hawking bag. I put fresh batteries in Harley's telemetry transmitter and checked the weather for weird high or low pressure systems. I weighed Harley twice to be sure her weight was right.

We were on the road at dawn and through the gate that keeps gun hunters off my hawking ground by seven o'clock. I drove right to the center of the grounds and parked the pickup. Just over a shallow rise the land flattened to uniform wheat grass and green needle grass. There are almost always grouse somewhere in the five-hundred-acre basin that stretches out to the north. The trick was finding them and getting them pointed.

Spud knew where we were even before I let him out. He'd been stiff that morning as I hustled up our breakfasts, but he showed no sign of infirmity when I opened his kennel door. He headed right for the basin that he knew was over the rise and I had to call him back a half-dozen times as I strapped on my hawking bag and talked Harley onto my fist. When I gave Spud the sign, he took off like it was the breakaway at the National Finals. By the time I got to where I could see the basin, he was two hundred yards out and working into the wind with his tail ringing. He looked good at that distance and it seemed that he had already determined there were no grouse in the eighty acres of rippling grass between us. If we were in New Brunswick there could be a hundred woodcock and two dozen ruffed grouse between us. There would also be a million board feet of lumber between us and it would seem like Spud was in the next county.

Sometimes sharptails are jumpy. You can flush them from a hundred yards away, so I stood still and let Spud work things out. He was almost a quarter of a mile away when a bird bumped in front of him. If it had been Melville who bumped the bird I would have had to run him down and make him whoa. But Spud's training days were over. It was an honest mistake; he knew his business and stopped only long enough to look back at me and make sure I wasn't angry. But when he started forward, two more grouse flushed.

They were in one of their spooky moods, and this time when Spud stopped, his tail spun. I was sure there were more birds in front of him but they were going to be too jumpy to get pointed without help. It's a risky operating procedure but sometimes you have to go with intuition. I struck Harley's hood just as a fourth grouse jumped. It was a good quarter mile off but she saw it immediately.

There was no chance of catching that grouse, but the wild flush had gotten Harley's blood up and let her know what we were doing. She climbed steadily toward where Spud stood waiting for her to pin the birds for him. I ran along behind. When I was a hundred yards from Spud I sent him on with a shouted "All right." Harley was five hundred feet above me now and still climbing to a position above Spud. There was no chance I'd flush the grouse at that distance with Harley in the air, so I eased up and let Spud work ahead.

It seemed like Harley had been up forever, and I watched for the first sign that she might be losing interest. If she started to leave, I was going to throw the pigeon for her. But she stayed intense and kept going higher. Spud localized his search. He worked carefully left, then back to the right. I began to kick myself. I'd screwed up. There were no more birds. Then Spud jerked into the breeze and froze. "Whoa, boy. Easy." I was jogging to catch up, glancing skyward to keep Harley in sight. She was very high and right above Spud. She was in perfect position and I wanted the grouse to come up before she turned, but I was still fifty yards away. There was no way I could flush it.

I don't know what happened for sure but, with Harley so high above them, I have a hard time believing the grouse left on their own. Maybe Spud bumped them by mistake, but I like to think he noticed that Harley was in perfect position and saw no reason to wait for me.

There were two of them, and when they came up I stopped running. I had a ringside seat. They lined out crosswind toward the west, but Harley had started her stoop at the first feather flick. She was too high to hit them until they had traveled fifty yards, but when she did, she smacked the last bird with enough force to crumple it in midair. The sound of the strike got to me just as the grouse hit the ground. It bounced four feet and Harley came in on it the same way she'd come in on the grouse that hit the wire.

One of the things that makes me love sharptails so passionately is their courage. There was a scuffle on the ground and the grouse got away. It didn't cower the way a pheasant or a partridge would. It exploded back into the air and rocketed toward the south as if nothing had happened.

I'd seen it happen a thousand times. Usually the falcon stays on the ground, clinging to a clump of feathers she hopes is the grouse. Occasionally, she will jump up and give chase.

That's what Harley did.

At this point it depends on how much damage was done in the stoop. If the falcon detects an injury she will push very hard and sometimes catch the grouse in the first cover it comes to. Usually the grouse beats the falcon to safe cover and the falcon comes back a few minutes later, hoping you'll flush another bird for her.

But Harley didn't come back. I waited with Spud for ten minutes with mixed feelings about whether I wanted to see her wing-ing her way toward us. It had been a fine flight, kill or no kill, and I wanted her back. The thought of losing her was deadening. But if she didn't return, it might mean she was on the grouse in the brush of a draw a quarter mile to the south. It would mean she had caught a grouse in acceptable style. Spud lay down in the dry wheat grass and we watched and waited another five minutes. When she didn't come back I figured there was a fifty-fifty chance she'd caught the grouse in the buffalo berry patch I know well. I made myself believe she was plucking the grouse and wondering when I would come to pick her up. I'd had falcons kill grouse in those buffalo berry bushes before. But if she wasn't there, the grouse had won and she was lost. I tried not to consider that possibility.

I didn't bother going back to the truck for the telemetry receiver. I made a beeline for the edge of the brush. That walk took another five minutes. I stood on the edge of the bushes with my good ear into the wind to listen for Harley's bell. Nothing. I knew that if she wasn't there, each minute could be taking her farther away. I walked through the brush and looked hard for grouse feathers, but I found nothing. I'd wasted another fifteen minutes.

By the time I got back to the truck and drove to the top of the draw where the receiver would work best, forty-five minutes had elapsed. I held the receiver to my ear and swung the antenna first in the direction I had last seen her, then through three hundred and sixty degrees of prairie. Still nothing. My heart felt swollen in my chest but this was no time to bog down. Harley was out there somewhere; and the longer she was gone, the less likely it was that I'd get her back. I drove to the next draw and tried the receiver again. There was no signal there either. The wind was picking up and I tried not to think that it was just such a current that peregrines like to migrate on. By then it was almost ten o'clock. I had unhooded her at eight-thirty. If she caught a thermal and the winds aloft were right, she could be halfway to Nebraska.

Since telemetry works on line of sight, I drove to a hill a mile to the west. I waved the antenna back and forth over our entire hawking ground. No signal. If the radio was working, she was nowhere near. Maybe the equipment was malfunctioning.

I went back and walked the draw where I still hoped she had caught the grouse. I longed to find her in a pile of grouse feathers. She was a slow eater and liked to pluck her game completely, but even if she had caught the grouse she would not stick around forever. If she took a full crop she wouldn't be hungry and might be very hard to get back. All this went through my mind as I searched for her. But it was no use; she had to have flown out of the area. I put Spud in his kennel in the back of the truck and headed for the nearest gravel road.

The Rapid City airport is eighteen miles from where I lost her but the roads are gravel and rough. It was one o'clock by the time I got there and another hour before I could get a plane and pilot rented. It took more time to tape the receiver's antenna to the wing strut and explain to the pilot what I wanted him to do.

"Come off the runway and climb out to the northeast. The higher we go, the more area we cover."

My plan was to climb to twelve thousand feet right over the hawking grounds. If we didn't get a signal, we'd fly a back-and-forth grid in a wedge shape to the south for a hundred miles. If we didn't get a signal by then, it would be all over.

I was numb as we lifted off the runway. Drills like this are in the category of "last-ditch efforts" and I saw my plans for the fall flying south on the wings of maybe the best bird I'd ever had. I sat slumped in the right seat wearing earphones plugged into the receiver. Nothing but engine noise and static. We climbed through five thousand feet and I pointed to the horizon where I thought I'd lost her.

More static and engine noise and the pilot wanted to ask a question. I took the earphones off to hear him. Yes, we were heading about right. When I put the earphones back on I thought I heard a beep. But it was only one and it could have been static. Then I thought I heard another one. I sat up. I held the earphone hard against my good ear, then tuned the receiver. Another faint beep.

I kept my eyes on the gauges and elbowed the pilot. I spun my finger for a pylon turn to the right. He understood perfectly and began to execute. He had only turned forty degrees when the gauges began to pop. The beep began to come steadily. I retuned, asked the pilot for a few more degrees to the right, and bingo, she was somewhere straight ahead.

I looked out at a thousand miles of South Dakota prairie stretched out far below us. When I found the hawking ground it looked tiny, and we were not pointed directly into it but south. I told the pilot to nose it down. It was midafternoon and if there was going to be any chance of finding her before dark we were going to have to pinpoint her soon. I'd already asked the pilot about landing in a pasture. His insurance wouldn't allow anything but asphalt under the wheels. It would take at least an hour to get back to the airport and drive to wherever she was.

We lost altitude, adjusting left or right as the receiver indicated, until we were a hundred feet off the ground. The signal was strong now, and I had to lower the volume. I'd just figured out that we were four miles south of where Harley had last been seen when suddenly the beep began getting fainter. I spun my finger for another turn and when we'd made a hundred and eighty degrees the beep came back. We had passed right over her.

I checked the landscape below: a flat draw with a few small bushes, a cattle watering tank, a fence line running west. "Follow the fence," I said.

We flew low for a half mile and the fence came to a cattle trail. We took the cattle trail to a shed. A gravel road ran past the shed. We followed the road for a quarter mile and I recognized a ranch house. To the west there was only an inch of sky between the sun and the horizon. "Home," I said. "Red-line this sucker."

The pilot was getting into this. He asked the tower for permission to make a straight-in approach. It was granted and we taxied right up to my truck at twenty miles an hour. I jumped out of the airplane and into the truck. I fishtailed on every gravel turn, but I found where the fence line met the cattle trail before the sun was completely down. I checked the telemetry once before I started jogging east. The signal wasn't loud, but I had one!

When I came to the rim of the draw, I took a minute to catch my breath. It was good to have a signal—it meant I was close to the transmitter—but I was gripped with the dread that something had happened to Harley, that the transmitter was attached to a dead and mangled falcon. It was still light enough to see where I was going without a flashlight, so I moved quickly. The signal got louder. I turned the volume way back to get maximum directional sensitivity. I walked over a flat of buffalo grass. I turned the volume down even more and with no background noise another sound came to me. It was the pure silver sound of a falcon bell.

There she was, not thirty feet in front of me. She stood tall in the short grass. She was safe but looked misshapen, and the area around her was white, as if snow had been falling all afternoon. When I got closer, I saw that the snow was feathers, a blanket of beautiful grouse feathers, and the huge lump at Harley's neck was a crop packed full of deep red meat.

I was afraid she would be hard to pick up, but she chipped and jumped to my fist. She must have spent the whole day wondering where I was. She feaked her beak on my glove and seemed glad when the hood slid over her head. There was nothing left of the grouse but bones, but I put them in my bag to show Erney.

FEAK. A stropping action used by birds to clean their beaks on a perch or the glove.

Later, I figured out that the draw I had found Harley in started three miles north, about a quarter mile from where I last saw her. I'd never known a falcon to chase a grouse three and a quarter miles. I'd never heard of a grouse not finding cover in the first mile. All I could figure was that Harley had pushed him the whole way, not allowing him enough space to put in. I tried to imagine what that flight must have been like. I had seen the beginning and gotten in on the end, but the texture of that long dash down the draw would always remain the stuff of dreams. The twists, the turns, the strategies for achieving cover, the strategies for taking those options away, the minute calculations for wind, the tremendous speed would be forever only gossamer grist for my imagination. As I carried Harley along the fence line toward where I'd parked the pickup, the sunset shot spirals of pink over my path.

Hunter's Moon

I had already been sleeping a couple of nights a week on the deck but in the beginning of October I gave up my bed altogether. I traded my habit of reading before falling asleep for a half hour of staring at the sky. Anyone who questions his heredity as a hunter should try lying supine under a hunter's moon as Orion swings up in the southeast. The harvest moon that occurs a month before might make you think of string beans and melons but this moon gives people the urge to howl and run naked through the night.

When I use the term "hunter," I mean it as distinct from a mere shooter and very different from someone who simply kills animals. Driving around in a pickup with semiautomatic weapons in search of deer is not hunting, and it's a shame that some people can't see the difference. When I am grouped with NRA cretins who use hunting season as an opportunity to prove something about their manhood, I shudder. I can only think that people who make that connection are unable to make the most basic distinctions among human behaviors. They are like aliens from outer space concluding that romantic love and rape are the same thing. To someone from a different planet the two acts might look similar but in the most important aspects, of course, they are opposite.

Whether they realize it or not, true hunters are practitioners of a kind of natural religion. Their church is the Great Outdoors and one of the sacraments is Hunting. I remember as a kid being told that everyone who believes in transubstantiation is really a cannibal. It was a way to malign Catholics. True hunters are defamed in a similar way by stories of wanton slaughter. There is an enormous difference between the Joe Six-Packs of the world and the growing numbers of people who view hunting as an activity rooted deep in all life and who hunt, at least partially, as a way of earning genuine organic nutrition. People might see hunting more clearly if they spent a week with a group of these true hunters. It might all make sense if they could come along on our annual woodcock hunt.

But, of course, the only people who come along already have a pretty good idea of what this trip is about. Charles Gaines is the force behind the expedition. He spent a long time researching the hunt and finally figured out how it could be done successfully and with grace. The group varies from year to year but Charles tries to keep the number to a reasonable level. New people are only invited if one of the old-timers dies or becomes a public embarrassment. (The place Kris and I occupy once belonged to a man whose checks to the guides bounced and whose dog was less interested in hunting than in humping hunting boots.)

That equinox autumn the group consisted of Charles; Melisse and Chris Child; Becky and Ed Gray; and Kris and me. We planned to meet our guides (a New Brunswick requirement) at a motel on the northeastern coast of the province. Kris had the week off and planned to pick up Melville and me in Boston, on the way to the coast of Maine and into Canada.

I usually fly through Denver, but since it has become a black hole for luggage and Melville was considered luggage, I went through Minneapolis. That change put me into Boston's Logan Airport at exactly the time I try to avoid—rush hour—and after two months of peace and quiet, it was truly a descent into the belly of the beast. If, after death, you have to serve time in hell, I'm convinced you get credit for time spent at Logan. If you've been there with a dog, it's time and a half.

I suffer around crowds. Once, years ago, in this same airport over Christmas vacation I panicked and broke from the sea of humanity and out through a door marked EMERGENCY EXIT ONLY. An alarm went off but I didn't care. Like a rodeo bull, I needed to be outside quick. I was leaning with my hands on a baggage cart, trying to get my heart back to normal by slowing my breathing, when a security guard came up behind me. "Hold it right there," he said. I have no idea if he had a gun drawn or not. It wouldn't have mattered. "You're not going back inside," he said.

"You're right about that," I said.

"You're going to stay right out here in the cold until that crowd clears."

I nodded, but inside I was saying something like: "Oh no, mister security guard, whatever you do, don't throw me in the briar patch."

It only took a couple of minutes to explain my way out of that one but I never forgot the feeling that sent me bursting out onto the tarmac. It was Calcutta Syndrome: an intense sense of panic brought on by too many people in one place. It is well known to westerners who have actually experienced an entire day without seeing or hearing another human being—and enjoyed it.

Calcutta Syndrome hit as soon as I got off the airplane. I was having trouble forcing myself to walk through the jetway toward the terminal. Luckily, Kris was waiting, and nothing could have kept me from her. We embraced and I held her doubly tight. When she pulled her head back and looked close at my face, she saw I was about to break and run. "Come on. Let's get you outside," she said.

The pressure eased slightly when I pushed through the doors in front of the baggage claim. Kris got my bags and waited for Melville to come out through a back door. I could occasionally see her through the crowd. When the back door opened and she bent over to say hi to Melville, I closed my eyes and dived back inside. Kris had Melville on a lead and one of my bags over a shoulder when I got to them. I took the second bag and, dragging the sky kennel, we ran for the door.

We found the car, loaded everything, and made our way through the dark, crumbling Callahan Tunnel, which leads to the city. There is a terrible intersection just beyond the tunnel that has scared me since I was a young man. There are stop signs and signals but nobody pays any attention to them. The year before, Chris Child was with us and because he is an old hand at this intersection, he piloted us through. "The main thing is not to hesitate," he said as he accelerated through a stop sign and squeezed between two cars. I had my eyes closed but opened them to judge how angry he had made the driver behind us. The guy looked enraged, but not at us—more a general rage. Chris had pulled right through like it was his highway, so now I did the same. To my surprise, there was no collision. Five minutes later, we were in a long line of cars heading north to Maine.

I found a nice place in line, set the cruise control at fifty-five, and stayed there between a minivan and a Mercedes. Things were cool and Kris started to talk. She told me about one of her patients, Little Darryl. He was two and a half years old and had a kind of cancer that might very well kill him. His lungs were shot but they could regenerate. He'd had chemotherapy, and most of his hair was gone. I could tell that Kris had become attached. "He's such a cute kid," she said, shaking her head.

I watched Kris from the corner of my eye and recognized the same expression of concern I'd seen for a dozen years. That concern was cutting lines into her face that some might see as unattractive. But they were beautiful to me because I knew she was earning them. I knew what they cost. If Darryl were to die in Kris's care he would be remembered forever in a new line at the corner of one of her eyes.

"Okay," I said. "No shop talk. Your job for this week is to hunt woodcock, to forget that you work at a hospital." I called back to Melville in the dog box. "Did you hear that, Melville? Woodcock. No shop talk."

"He's ready," Kris said.

"Me too."

"Oh, yeah?" Kris said. "Ready for what?"

I reached over and pulled her closer. "A week in New Brunswick with you," I said.

We traveled a couple of hours into the night, then stayed in a cheap motel, with Melville fighting most of the time to establish himself on the bed between us. "What's he think he is?" I asked.

"A police dog. Attached to the vice squad."

"Go on, Mel, get out of here."

We got a reasonable start in the morning, but it takes forever to cross New Brunswick against the grain and we didn't make Fonteneux's Motel until six o'clock. Dinner reservations were for seven-thirty; we still had a good hour and a half for cocktails and hellos.

The cocktails and hellos were already under way when we pulled around to the back of the motel where Mr. Fonteneux always puts us. It was easy to see why he doesn't want any of us out front where his other customers can see. The area around our group's five rooms was a sea of wagging tails and wool shirts. The tailgate of the Grays' jeep was down and a couple of bottles of scotch balanced precariously as dogs jumped up and down in a combination of play and pecking-order politics. Everyone was there, including our two guides, Gordy and Bill, and their four springers. I picked Moose's mother out of the pack easily. She looked just like her daughter and trotted around with a high head, like the matriarch troll she is.

We shook hands with everyone and hugged all around. Melisse handed us drinks and the dogs gathered to say hello to Melville. Chris and I had met in the summer to do a little fishing in the Rockies but it had been a year since we had seen any of the others. There was a lot to talk about and the cocktailgate party bled right into the dining room, where most of us began with a mound of mussels steamed somehow in Pernod.

There was wine with an unpronounceable name and then, since I'd been starved for seafood, I followed Bill and Gordy's lead and ordered scallops and sole broiled in lemon sauce with sugar peas. Kris and Charles had the veal. The Childs ordered two kinds of pasta; Melisse's included hot peppers. Oysters appeared and made the rounds. Ed Gray finally settled on the sea bass and Becky ordered something I'd never heard of. Forks crisscrossed the table marauding a scallop here, a bite of squash there. More wine came. Then crème brûlée, coffee, and brandy.

It was good to be back in the Northwoods.

Each morning we got our marching orders. By eight o'clock Charles would have cleared a table in the café and rolled out a map. He was forever in deep consultation with Bill and Gordy. He pointed to the crosshatched covers and traced out routes to reach them with the confidence of a Colin Powell. Charles had been hunting New Brunswick for decades and knew the terrain as well as did any native. He's a woodcock aficionado of the highest order. He studies the sport and has kept a running log of each day in the alders for years and years. He remembers every flush.

Because woodcock covers are continually evolving from nascent, to prime, to gone by, it is necessary to keep looking for new ones. Charles takes the long view of woodcock hunting and, to ensure that it is always good, assigns one car to reconnaissance duty each day. The people are rotated from car to car and divided up according to dog power—puppies with experienced dogs, dogs who need fine tuning to special spots.

Woodcock hunting is about habitat, natural history, and dogs. The focus of the hunt is a small, migratory bird with habits and characteristics of flight that are utterly charming. They settle into quiet alder runs and golden poplar stands on their way south and probe the soft earth for worms with their long, flexible beaks. Dogs love them and no bird holds better under a point.

The experience of shooting woodcock over a point is so rewarding and such a conservative use of the resource that I have always felt it's a shame to shoot them any other way. If I walk up a woodcock, or particularly if a dog bumps one, I don't shoot. My hope is that the bird might flutter into the cover ahead and give us another chance to draw all the elements of the hunt together. Kris and I try to walk slowly, leaving the guns broken much of the time, tuning into the autumn woods and listening for Melville's bell to go silent. When it does, we move quickly to flank the dog. We try to keep one of us alternately in the open as we move to Melville's sides. When we are close and in reasonable position to shoot, we stand and savor the moment. We praise Melville and try to give him the impression that we are honoring his point, which in a way we are. The ultimate is to get in a position where you can see the bird under the dog's nose. Sometimes one is crouched on a patch of bare dirt, sometimes it blends into the dry leaves so well that the first thing you see is a shiny black eye.

One magic day in Melville's first year, our guide took us to a tiny stand of poplar and fir along a river. It was a half-mile walk through woods that, to me, were indistinguishable from the stand he had in mind. I asked him what the difference was and he said our destination was a cover and the rest wasn't. It all seemed too old to me, with trees that were tall enough to keep the forest floor dark and the blue sky remote. But the guide was right. We moved twenty birds in a five-acre cover. There was a woodcock every hundred feet, and Spud, who was at the height of his powers that year, made points on two doubles and a triple—the first and last triple I've ever seen. I can't remember if we shot any of those birds. It didn't matter. I remember that place as something from the land of Oz, with beautiful little batlike birds floating up through dark tree branches toward the light above.

A few days into the hunt we spent a day at the hunting and fishing lodge of a Toronto sportsman named Steve Latner. I don't know how Charles does it but everywhere he goes he manages to scam an invitation to a first-rate dinner, even in the wilds of New Brunswick.

Latner's Sevogle Lodge is run by a maniac named Frenchy. The story goes that Steve had been salmon fishing on the Miramichi River and drew Frenchy for his guide. It started to rain as they headed down the river and Frenchy began to swear. They dug out their foul-weather gear and Frenchy's turned out to be a Kmart raincoat that was already torn in several places. They took off again with Steve hunkered in the middle of the boat and Frenchy standing in the rear, cursing the gods, with one hand on the outboard's arm. The wind worked at the rips in his raincoat until it was nothing but shreds and Frenchy was drenched to the skin.

Frenchy and Steve didn't know each other so Steve didn't know what to expect when Frenchy stopped the boat and pulled his soaked shirt away from his chest. "You mind if I take this son of a bitch off?" Steve shrugged and Frenchy took that as permission. A minute later they were roaring down the Miramichi into the oncoming rain with Steve sitting dazed on the middle seat and Frenchy at the helm, buck naked except for his knee-high rubber boots.

Steve immediately put him on the payroll. Although it might have been an impulsive hiring, it was brilliant. With Steve's guidance and high standards, Frenchy and his girlfriend, Chantelle, run a top-notch outfit for select salmon fishermen, Steve, and, luckily for our group, Steve's friends. The Sevogle Lodge lays the best table in all the Maritimes and the setting and company are worldclass.

We'd been hunting all morning. It was a typical cool, overcast New Brunswick day and we'd worked up an appetite. When we stopped to eat a sandwich and candy bar at a gas station, Kris wistfully began to speculate about what Steve might have for dinner. Bill and Gordy were friends of Frenchy's and had gotten the word that preparations had been under way for days. "Maybe he'll do wild game," Kris said.

We sat under the back door of the Explorer. Melville was a young dog and had worked hard that morning. He was between us in his sky kennel, catching a nap and paying no attention to our conversation. "I hope it's a big chunk of meat with some thick French sauce," I said.

"No, it'll be some kind of bird. Cornish hens, maybe ducks."

"Maybe we'll get asparagus."

"Yeah, asparagus. And soup. Some kind of chowder."

"No. Cold soup. Pumpkin or squash."

My ham-and-cheese sandwich didn't look so good. I'd been carrying it in my game bag all morning. I opened up Melville's kennel door to give it to him just as a local walked by. When he saw Melville, he came over. "I just love dogs," he said.

I was holding the sandwich out to Melville but his head was still down. He tried to look up to where he was getting good scent, but he was tired and his face was too heavy. All we could see was the red under his eyeballs. The man jumped back. "Ah, poor old bugger. Lost his eyes, did he?" Just then Melville raised his head to take the sandwich gently. First the whites, then the pupils rolled into view. "Oh." The man reached out and rubbed Melville's head. "Poor old bugger."

We hunted a lovely little cover on our way to the Sevogle Lodge and I got to watch Kris and Melville move along the edge of a half-dozen neglected apple trees at the back of an old homestead. Melville was birdy and so was Kris. They went steadily ahead, Melville staying downwind and Kris moving to openings in the cover where she could get a shot if a bird came up. Kris shoots a pretty little Beretta 28-gauge and shoots it well. I was sure there was a ruffed grouse ahead of them and when the bird broke from in front of Mel, Kris took a ninety-degree passing shot and crumpled it in front of Melville's charge. He caught it on the bounce and came walking back to Kris with a silly look of embarrassed pride. We spent some time praising Melville and I praised Kris. We all praised the grouse. I held it in my hand. Even though it was a big male, it was still only three-quarters the size of a sharptail, and I thought how much more delicate it was. It was a fine red-phase grouse and its feathers matched Melville's orange belton coat as if the colors were chosen from an artist's palette.

It was dark as we wound our way through the woods to the buildings on the edge of the Sevogle River gorge. Steve, Frenchy, a

Brittany spaniel, and a springer came out to greet us. There were handshakes, tail wags, hugs, and sniffs. We stowed our gear, cleaned up, and started in on the single-malt scotch. I am always amazed how people I know to be exhausted and half nuts can rise to the occasion and act absolutely civilized. Take Bill and Gordy, for instance. Two nights before, they were lying on their motel room beds in their underwear yelling at a hockey game and drinking Seagram's from the bottle. That night they were wearing sweaters, sipping Macallan's from snifters, and debating the merits of Canadian versus U.S. health care.

The women were luminescent. Their mere presence gave the lodge a measure of elegance. Steve was a literature major in college and kept Charles, Ed, and me struggling to remember the plot of *Swann's Way*. Did it have a plot? But Chris silenced him with the pronouncement that he was the only living human being in Utah to have read all of Churchill's histories. Melisse rolled her eyes. "He's so much fun," she said.

Then came the hors d'oeuvres: salmon on one plate, medium-rare woodcock breast on the other, all sliced thin and fancy on tiny pieces of bread and sprinkled with herbs. The talk moved to birds and bird dogs and the talkers moved to the table, where we found a corn-and-black-bean soup and a lobster salad that could cause anyone to write a bad check. The wine had been breathing while we talked. It was rich, smoky, and plentiful. The table looked more like a work of art than a platform from which to eat.

Steve had the women placed strategically and I had an opportunity to watch Kris across the table. She glowed, and the health in her face reminded me how much nicer hunting and fishing is when it's coed. We'd had a wonderful day in the field. Melville had hunted and pointed well. Kris had shot well. She was delighted and it showed.

Next came a rack of lamb with twice-baked potatoes. The vegetable included sliced white truffles. The only other time I had eaten truffles was in a soup, and a magnifying glass was needed to find them. These babies were as big as tennis balls. They had been passed around before they were prepared and they smelled of real life, thick and sensual. Once they were mixed with lightly steamed carrots and julienned zucchini, it didn't take long to appreciate their musty taste. The merlot made it once more around the table, then magically was replaced with port and an ice wine made from frozen grapes. Then came imported ice cream, cheese, fruit, and deep dark coffee.

Before we went to bed, Kris and I took a walk in the cold night air. All the dogs had been banished from the lodge and we thought Melville might wonder what had happened to us. I told Kris how much I'd been missing her. I told her how special Harley was. I told her Harley was capable of the best flights I'd ever seen. I told her I felt on the verge of something significant. I confessed that I saw my-self in the autumn of my life, and that I needed to achieve some things with Harley that I never had achieved before. But I didn't con-fess that I'd begun to consider staying in South Dakota for the entire winter.

We were standing on the edge of the Sevogle gorge. After I spoke, the sound of the river tumbling from salmon pool to salmon pool filled the void. When she turned to me, she was shaking her head. "It must be a male thing," she said. "You think of the fall equinox and see a life seventy-five percent finished, a mountain of things that need doing. I see equal periods of light and dark, day and night. I think of the heavens in balance." She shook her head again and looked into the dark gorge. "Got to be a male thing."

The sound of the river took over again and I wondered if salmon were moving upstream below us. I leaned and burrowed my face in Kris's hair. It smelled better than the truffles. In fact, everything smelled alive. We sniffed the frosty air as we walked and the breeze brought us the rich scent of a Maritime autumn.

When we checked on Melville, he refused to get out of his kennel. He was half on his back like a puppy and his paws were thrust upward. I had read in Michael Ondaatje's *The English Patient* that a dog's feet retain a trace of scent from everywhere he's been that day. I took up one of Melville's paws. Ondaatje was right. I could smell alder and black dirt, crushed maple leaves and pine needles. Kris took Melville's other paw and we both smelled poplar and stone, raspberry and primrose. We breathed deeply and caught the scent of woodcock and grouse. When we came to our senses, Melville was looking up at us like we'd lost our minds.

Kris began to think of work the day before we arrived back in New Hampshire. By the time we got to Bangor, Maine, she started wondering out loud how Little Darryl was doing. She was as engrossed in her life as I was in mine. I rationalized that living with her in New England while she was so busy wouldn't be that much different from living two thousand miles away.

I had to talk to Kris about my plans, but I put it off. I took the first day in Hanover to organize our gear. Everything was wet and dirty and I spent most of the morning washing and drying clothes. Melville lay around until noon but he got interested when I brought the guns out to clean them. By the next morning, he was scratching on the door, impatient to go hunting.

Chris and Charles had once lived close to Hanover and had given me a map to a cover that had been good to them. It was mid-October, about the time woodcock come through New Hampshire, and Melville was getting insistent with his scratching at the door, so I thought I'd give it a try. I was looking forward to getting out again, of course. It always takes my dogs a few days to adjust from prairie grouse to close country woodcock and it isn't until the end of the hunt that they get good. Melville was just then peaking. I longed for one more day in the field.

It's good to hunt with friends but it's also good to hunt alone. Things happen when it's just you and your dog that don't happen when there's someone else to see it. The dog is always brilliant when you're alone, you always shoot better, you see things that have never occurred before, and no one believes you. For that reason I try not to talk about days alone in the field, but this one was special.

It was warm for October but it was cold farther north and I hoped that was pushing woodcock down into New Hampshire, where the fall trees were now at their most colorful. In South Dakota the leaves have only three colors—green, yellow, and gone. As I followed the map to Charles and Chris's cover, I saw colors I'd only seen in magazines. They dazzled me and by the time I found the pulloff, I was itching to get into them. By then I figured that any woodcock would be just a bonus.

Melville poured out of his kennel and jumped into my arms. He stretched his neck out for me to snap the bell onto his collar. Melville is lanky, with long feathering under the tail and behind his legs. When he gets excited he leaps in rolling bounds. Erney calls him a galoot and describes his gait as a galumph. When Mel sees a shotgun he starts running in circles. If it takes too long to get under way, he sometimes sits at the gunner's side and paws his leg. That day in the New Hampshire woods he tore around the pickup, scooping fallen leaves up in his mouth and tossing them over his shoulder. By the time I got my gun together he was sitting two feet away, staring at me and making a sound like a comedian doing an impression of a canine news anchor.

"All right," I said, and he leaped into the air and took off for a small line of alders that ran downhill and between two banks of poplars. Once he was out thirty feet, he slowed to a shuffling trot that was easy to keep up with. We hadn't gone forty yards before he started to pussyfoot. He got low and stretched out. His brow furrowed with concentration and he froze up. It was fairly open and I was already within shotgun range, so I froze too. He seemed to swell up as if he were taking the bird's scent into his lungs but not letting it out. I was fifteen feet directly behind Melville and figured the woodcock to be under the alders in front of him. I took a step forward before I closed the shotgun and a bird came up three feet to my left. It surprised us both. Melville's head turned when it whistled into the air. I tried to close the gun and get a shot, but there was no time. Melville was staring at me. At first I thought he was wondering why I hadn't shot. "Sorry, boy," I apologized. But he slowly swiveled his head back to its original position. When I moved ahead of him, a second bird came up and I tapped him with the 20-gauge at the apex of his flush, just as he leveled off over the canopy.

Sometimes Melville retrieves and sometimes he doesn't. If he points the bird, and it goes down in front of him, the chances are good. This time he went right to it and brought it back at once. I got down on my knees to accept the bird and Melville, unlike Spud, who spits them out and tears off to find more, sat and appraised the bird with me. It was a beautiful big hen. I spread its delicate wings and tail to see the subtle black and brown markings. We looked at the improbably large head and eyes. I felt the texture of her long beak and I remarked how perfect she was.

Melville seemed to agree. He remained sitting until I had stowed the bird in my game bag and replaced the shell in the shotgun. We had barely begun to hunt the cover and already we'd started two birds. I had a feeling that we were into something good. It was a big cover with everything from apple trees to alders. It would be a perfect place to find a flight, a group of woodcock fresh in from the north.

As we got deeper into the cover, the bounce disappeared from Melville's gait. The hot day wasn't the problem. His face had that look of deep concern and I knew there was bird scent everywhere. He pointed two more birds before we got to the cover's first sweet spot. I didn't shoot at either of them. Now I was sure there would be more, and the limit was only three birds. I didn't want to get halfway through the cover and have to quit.

We started twenty-seven woodcock and two grouse that day. Melville bumped five woodcock and I bumped eight. Melville pointed both grouse and all the rest of the woodcock. By the time we came along the last beat of the cover, when the car was just ahead through the alders, he was one hot and tired dog. I had shot one of the grouse and two woodcock, so I could still shoot another woodcock if I wanted to. It looked like I wasn't going to get the chance, though. Melville's tongue hung out and he was moving slowly. Then, just as he started down through the marshy cut at the bottom of the alder run, his panting stopped and he stiffened into a point. It was the thickest part of the alders and Melville struck a classic pose as he stood rigid in the shadowy tangle. I knew he was exhausted and I wanted badly to shoot the bird for him; however, it was hard to get into a position where I could flush and shoot. He stayed solid as I struggled over and under the alders. It was taking forever. I got stuck and had to circle back. I was desperate to finish this season on a good note, so I tried another path to an opening. When I got stuck a second time I looked to Melville, expecting him to be impatient. He was still pointing but, as I watched, he slowly lowered himself. I thought he was sick, or maybe going to lie down on point. He kept his head up and his attention focused straight ahead until his muzzle was in the muddy water at his feet. Without blinking an eye he lapped at the water, then raised slowly back up to perfect pointing position.

That did it. I had to shoot the bird for him. I squeezed through a hole in the alders on my hands and knees and had just regained my feet when the bird whistled up. I had one shot and I took it. To my amazement and Melville's joy, the bird folded and landed dead not twenty feet in front of us. Mel retrieved it and as I took it from his tender mouth I knew that next year he would take Spud's place. The pup had come of age.

The car seemed to float on the drive back to the house; as I turned onto our road, though, my thoughts shifted from that last marvelous day of woodcock hunting to the day ahead. Melville and I were supposed to be in Boston by six-thirty in the morning. We would miss rush hour so it wasn't the thought of a busy airport full of people that was making me suddenly anxious. I pulled into the driveway and looked for Kris's car in the garage. She was still at the hospital.

Leaving her again was part of what was nagging at me. But there was more. As I stowed my hunting gear and cleaned the shotgun it came to me that I felt guilty not only for leaving Kris but, also because, for the last ten days, I had not been flying Dundee, Alice, Little Bird, and, especially, Harley. This had been a sort of decadent vacation from responsibilities to which I had committed myself. Harley could easily be the best grouse hawk I had ever had and I had left her for almost two weeks during a critical time in her development. I had to resist calling Erney to see how she was doing.

As I brushed New England's burrs from Melville's coat, all I could think of was Harley. I would ride the airport shuttle early the next morning and be in South Dakota in less than twenty-four hours. My other life was coming hard into focus. For the last ten days I'd been suppressing my hopes for Harley. Now I admitted to myself that I wanted her to run up a score on grouse. I wanted her to fly high and hard clear into March. There was a sense that I would never again have a chance like this and I had to make the most of it.

By the time Kris arrived home I had cleaned the 20-gauge for the last time that season. I had also cleaned the three woodcock and the grouse. In a bowl on the kitchen counter, the grouse lay plucked and plump and the woodcock were cut into breasts and legs beside it. A bottle of Pinot Noir was decanting on the table. "Mel and I have done our job," I told Kris. "You can take over."

The grouse was stuffed with pancetta, sage, and garlic, then wrapped in foil. While it roasted, wild rice simmered and bits of pasta cooked. The woodcock was sautéed hot and fast in butter. Kris sipped some wine before she removed the woodcock and put it aside in a low dish. She seemed most interested in the residue that was left in the pan. In went cream and up went the heat until the sauce was thick. Then she poured it over the woodcock parts. "Hors d'oeuvres," she said.

Melville raised his head from the couch where he'd been sleeping. I shook my head: "Forget it, boy."

The woodcock was rich and delicious. We nibbled as I set the table and Kris stirred the pasta and rice together. Then we sat down to finish the woodcock and wait for the grouse to be done. She told me that Little Darryl had been released from the critical-care unit while she was gone but his lungs had filled again and now he was back. She had threaded a new tube into his heart that afternoon. I told her about Melville's brilliant performance but I couldn't muster the enthusiasm it deserved. I was thinking about Harley.

By the time the grouse and pilaf was ready, Kris knew I had something on my mind. She served up the meal, poured more wine, and sat down across from me. "So what's bothering you?" she asked.

"I'm not really sure," I said.

We ate the grouse in silence and each finished a glass of wine. "I'm thinking about staying in South Dakota a little longer than we talked about."

Kris didn't look at me. She cut a piece of grouse breast and stabbed it with her fork. "It's lonely here," she said. "I could use someone to talk to."

"I know. But you're busy. I wouldn't see you that much anyway." She still wouldn't look at me.

"You can do what you want," she said.

"I don't want to do it if you don't want me to. What would you say if I stayed out there until March?"

She stopped playing with the grouse. "Do what you have to do," she said. Then she finally looked up at me. "But I'd say it was pretty shitty."

We left it unresolved. We held each other that night but we didn't talk about how long I'd stay in South Dakota. When Kris's alarm went off at five the next morning we got up and ready to leave like robots. She dropped Mel and me at the hotel in Hanover where we'd catch the shuttle for the airport. The best we could manage through the open car window was a peck on the cheek.

Erney again picked us up at the airport, but this time it was midday. My first question was, "How have the birds been flying?"

He gave me a long preamble about the poor weather. The wind had been out of the northwest and blowing in the twenty-mile-an-hour range almost every day. I knew what he was leading up to. "I only got the birds flown five days out of the ten," he said.

"And?"

"And Alice caught one little bird, but she ate it before I could identify it for sure. Probably a grasshopper sparrow."

"And?"

"I couldn't get Little Bird even to look at a duck." He was disgusted.

"And?"

"Harley?" The disgusted look turned to dumb innocence.

"Yeah, Harley."

"She caught two."

"Two what?"

He smiled and wiggled his eyebrows. "Grouse!"

"No."

"You bet. Just like we knew what we were doing."

"Good flights?"

"Finest kind."

We were on our way to the ranch and I surveyed the western sky. There was lots of daylight left but the last of the cottonwood leaves were dancing violently in the wind. I knew I should take that afternoon to cool out and get organized, but I was bit by the falconry bug. The first thing I did when I got home was go to the weathering yard and look at Harley. She stood on her block with her feathers fluffed and her eyes narrowed. Blood from yesterday's grouse was dried on her belly feathers, feet, and cere. She seemed bigger and even more confident than she had ten days before. I wanted her to look at me but she wouldn't. She kept her eyes on the horizon.

CERE. The soft skin at the base of the beak, usually yellow in adult birds of prey and a bluish green in immatures.

When I weighed the birds I found that Erney had done a good job. Little Bird, Dundee, and Alice were exactly where they should be, but because she had caught a grouse the day before, and because Erney believes in feeding a falcon up on a kill, Harley was too heavy to fly. I was disappointed. Because the wind was still strong, we would have to count on it dropping just before dark and probably there wouldn't be enough time to fly everyone anyway.

Since Little Bird hadn't made a kill for ten days, we decided to fly a release partridge instead of a duck to get her back in the swing of things. At four o'clock I took Alice on my fist and told Erney to load Spud and Little Bird in the pickup and meet me on The Bottom, where the release pens were. He shrugged and said it was still pretty windy. But I wasn't going to miss a day's flying. I planned to walk the edge of the section with Alice in hopes of flushing a dove and rendezvous with Erney in about forty-five minutes.

Two meadowlarks jumped as soon as I crossed the fence, but they must have been too far away because Alice didn't seem to notice them. Out in the open, the gusts were strong and I had to keep Alice pointed into them, but that put her at a decided disadvantage with birds flushing into the wind. Because wind also makes birds jumpy, the only doves we saw flushed wild, and Alice refused them. By the time I saw Erney coming down the hill I was frustrated, and when a dove flushed too far ahead, I tried to cast Alice off at it. That only served to frighten her and she spread her wings and let the wind take her downwind to a fence post. It took her longer than usual to come to the fist and I figured I'd better quit while I was ahead. I fed her up as we covered the last quarter of a mile to the pickup, with me sidling into the wind so Alice could eat on the fist in the lee of my body.

Erney was resting on the tailgate with Little Bird hooded on his fist. He stroked her and she bit at him in a perfunctory way, with only a halfhearted desire to connect. Behind him, Spud whined softly, thumping his tail against the kennel wall. This was Spud's favorite game, one he could go on playing for perhaps a few more years. We gave the wind another ten minutes to settle. As the sun touched the horizon in the west, the gusts began to die down. By the time I opened the door on the north side of the recall pen the wind was blowing no more than ten miles per hour.

As soon as the door opened, eight partridge shot into the air and out. They flew in a covey toward the north. They flew and flew, finally disappearing about a quarter of a mile away, into a depression in the alfalfa field. I studied the horizon on the far side of the depression with the binoculars for a full minute and didn't see the birds top the rise. They had to be somewhere there, a wonderful spot to fly them.

We waited another few minutes to let them settle in and lay down some scent, then put Little Bird up to freeze them. We turned old Spud loose. He hit the ground running. Even though his bad leg touched down only about half the time, he lined out for the depression. Erney and I looked at each other and shook our heads. For years, Spud's ability to know where the birds are had amazed us. Spud had been in the kennel when I had released the partridge, so he couldn't have seen which direction they went and couldn't have had any idea how far they had flown. But there he was, already a hundred yards out and running right for the birds.

Erney and I didn't know exactly where they were, of course, and neither did Spud. He had to take enough time to quarter through the alfalfa leading up to the depression, but Erney and I were still far behind when Spud disappeared at exactly the place the partridge had disappeared fifteen minutes before. Little Bird, doing her thing, was probably seven hundred feet high by the time we got to where we could see into the depression.

There was Spud, tail high and nose into the wind. We paused on the high ground sixty yards from the point and let Little Bird get a little more altitude. She and Spud had done this a hundred times; she knew exactly what was going to happen. She was good at this—too good, perhaps. She was wed to these partridge. It was what she did for a living. Though the flights were nice, they were predictable and the birds were really only half wild. I felt a little bored with it as I made my way to the upwind side of the point.

Erney moved to Spud's side to remind the old fool that he wasn't a flushing spaniel and I walked downwind into the covey. They came up as one and gave Little Bird a crosswind shot. She used her standard technique—folding completely, stooping hard until she nearly hit the ground, then coming up into the birds. This was almost always lethal: The partridge couldn't outfly her, so, by being below them, she had taken away their only escape route. The covey had covered only about seventy yards when she came up through them and out the other side with a plump hen in her talons.

I watched the rest of the covey with my binoculars. They flew for nearly a mile before they put in on a sage flat near a stock pond. I should have been more interested in Little Bird and her kill, but just then the rest of the covey fascinated me more. Even from a mile away I knew they would be back in the pen by noon the next day.

That night I sipped my brandy and rubbed the dog's ears and let my mind race. I should have been thinking about walking the fields with Alice in the cool afternoons. I should have been trying to understand how to convince Little Bird that she should fly ducks as hard as she did release partridge. I should have been thinking about Kris. Instead I was thinking about Harley. I was wondering how many grouse she might be able to catch in the next four months.

I was up early the next morning driving the gravel roads and glassing the edges of wheat fields. I didn't have a falcon with me but I had all the dogs. Erney had only flown Harley in one place. It was a good place, grouse were coming in every day, but I wanted more than one slip a day. My dreams the night before had been nothing but one powerful stoop after another. It was always Harley; the quarry was always grouse.

To save the setters I ran Spud at one place and Melville at the next. Moose rode in her smaller kennel. When I had surveyed all the local grouse spots and found that about half of them were being used, I worked her on pigeons in a hay field a mile from the ranch.

BIDDABLE. Trainable, willing to obey.

She was still a little timid but very biddable and would take hand signals and range up to thirty yards. I left her in the pickup, planted the pigeons, then let her out, directing her to them with hand signals and commands. If she was quick, she would catch the pigeon before it got out of the grass and retrieve it. She would let me take it from her mouth as if it were a shot bird. If it got away from her, we treated it like a flushed bird and I made her hup.

She was not quite confident enough to use to flush grouse under a falcon. When a falcon is in the air, the dogs are relegated to the sideshow, and sometimes they don't get the attention they need. They can pick up bad habits quickly. Moose might misunderstand the tension I'd give off trying to get the slip just right and feel it as pressure. But she was catching on and I was sure she would do us some good yet that season.

While searching for grouse, I would come across ponds holding ducks. It was late October, traditionally our best time for ducks, and there was an array of species. The majority were medium-sized ducks: gadwalls, wigeon, shovelers. There were a few teal left on the smaller ponds and a smattering of mallards and pintails recently down from somewhere farther north. We seldom get divers but that morning I even saw some scaup. It was a duck hawker's paradise and I promised myself to fly Little Bird at a gadwall or a wigeon. But even as I was promising myself, I felt a touch of annoyance at having to take time away from Harley to fly a duck.

The days had shortened considerably. Erney told me it was dark by five-fifteen, so we started flying birds right after lunch. There was wind, not like the day before, though, and I was able to get Alice much closer to the few doves that were still around. But she didn't catch a dove. The slips weren't good enough to inspire her. I was wasting time, so we started back toward the ranch.

A quarter of a mile from the house a meadowlark jumped from my feet and she plucked it out of the air like so much feathery meat. It was a nice flight and I felt some of the same amazement I'd felt when she'd caught that first dove. Still, it should have affected me more. I should have savored the experience, but I was impatient to get to a particular spot where I knew grouse would be coming in, so I hurried her on her kill.

Making in too quickly or awkwardly is a stupid thing to do. It excites the bird and, if done repeatedly, can ruin its manners and make it unpleasant to fly. When I reached in to pick her up, Alice mantled over the lark. She hopped away and I should have just let her go. I should have chilled out, watched the clouds, and in ten minutes tried her again. Instead, I grabbed a jess to keep her where she was, and that made things even worse. Finally I had to do what I should have done at the beginning. I backed away and let her relish her meal. By then I was angry with myself and any chance of enjoying the rest of the afternoon was gone.

When I got back to the house, Erney had the two game hawks hooded and loaded into the truck. All three dogs were loaded too and we got rolling as soon as I'd put Alice in the weathering yard. Dundee was there on his perch. I tossed him a piece of food; there wouldn't be time to fly him that night.

The pond I had planned to fly with Little Bird was vacant. There had been a nice raft of ducks on it earlier but now they were gone. A cloud bank was building in the west and threatening a premature sunset. We raced to the next pond and lucked out. There would still be time to fly both birds if Little Bird didn't fool around. "You're asking a lot," said Erney. "Fooling around is what she does best."

Erney's prediction turned out to be on target. Little Bird went up all right, but she drifted a quarter of a mile away from the pond, and no matter what we did, she wouldn't come back to wait on. She careened back and forth at a great altitude, but always downwind. Finally I got fed up and flushed the ducks when there was no possible way she could catch up to them. She didn't even try. I called her down to a lure garnished with nothing but a chicken foot. She'd just earned herself a membership to the avian Weight Watcher's program.

By the time we got to the sorghum field where I wanted to fly Harley, it was darker than I would have liked. Grouse often come into a grainfield at the end of the day and that morning I'd discovered that they'd been using this one. But we didn't know if they were in the field yet. They could have come in while we were waiting for Little Bird to get serious. The sorghum was too thin to hold them for a point unless Harley was already in the air. There was no sense in running the setters. I'd planned to be there in time to see them fly into the field. Now we'd have to find them on the ground or it would be strictly flying on speculation—a practice that risks disappointing the falcon and, in time, can ruin her.

We parked the truck on the gravel road and began glassing the field. The stubble was short, maybe six inches, and the rows ran north and south. We were looking east. That meant any grouse that showed itself would have to stick its head above the stubble. To the naked eye the field looked trim as a carpet, but it was thinner cover than it seemed. When I brought up the binoculars, it was instantly clear that this particular farmer's combine had left several thousand sorghum heads. A sorghum head looks a lot like a grouse head, so every one had to be checked out for movement or eyes. Erney and I settled in.

The sun was setting. The stubble, fringed with its own shadows, was mesmerizing. I rolled down the window to listen for grouse talking in the field. Nothing. Then Erney poked me. "Right in line with the southeast corner post. What is that?"

I swung to the corner post, then down. It was a long way away, nearly half a mile, and I couldn't tell if the deviation in the stubble was grain or grouse. I brought the spotting scope out from under the seat, clipped it to the window, and twisted the darker spots into focus. It took a moment to get things just right, but as soon as the focus was perfect, the dinosaur-like head of a sharptail was obvious. There was a movement behind it and another head came up. Then what I had thought was a sorghum head became a third grouse. "Got 'em," I said. "Just in front of that corner post and to the left. Strung out for thirty yards. Probably the whole bunch."

"That corner dried out," Erney said. "The stubble is real thin. Tough to get them pointed."

He was right. That particular part of the field was poor soil. It didn't hold water and the crop had been sparse. A pointing dog would bust them, but they'd bust in their own time—just when Harley was out of position. She'd stoop at the grouse that got up wide and when she was down, the rest of the flock would come up. It was a lousy slip for a setter. "We'll have to loose the Moose," I said, though I knew she wasn't ready.

Spud and Melville took it hard. Spud scratched wildly at his kennel door and Melville began a wail fit for an Irish wake. Moose pranced back and forth in front of them both. When she came off the tailgate her ears flared out like wings, as if she were a furry little Dumbo. The setters were crushed. I had to order them to shut up.

When the nights begin getting cold and the days shorter, falcons sometimes experience a spurt of maturity. They get hard the same way the grouse get hard. Everything gets faster, smarter, and the flight skills needed to kill or escape reach an almost unbelievable level. This is the time of year that separates the real game hawks from the birds that depend on the quarry making a mistake. I hadn't seen Harley fly for nearly two weeks and in those two weeks night frost had become the norm. The world had changed. The inferior grouse were dead. The rest had flocked up and were feeding mostly on grain. Any grouse that had made it to this last week in October had a decent chance to carry its genes into the next generation. These were not homing pigeons or release partridge. This was for real.

As soon as I took Harley's hood off, I knew she had felt those cold nights. It was in her black eyes, the way she refused to look at me, the way she scanned the horizon for movement. She roused without changing expression and took to the air, pumping into the wind until she was two hundred feet high. Only when she started her first turn did she set her wings, and then it was only for a second. Moose watched her but I let her know that Harley was on our side. She seemed to get it and walked as happily at heel as a twelve-inch dog, walking perpendicular to six-inch stubble, can.

The hike was too far for Erney, so he stayed at the truck. I made a beeline for the center point of the field and stopped still a quarter of a mile from the grouse. The wind was at my back. Harley was flying strong, in tight circles, maybe six hundred feet above us. I let her take a downwind swing, then started walking again. When we were a hundred yards from where I thought the grouse would be, I tried to make Moose believe that this was just like our pigeon game. But she'd felt that something was different and watched me for a clue. I leaned down and petted her and moved up another fifty yards.

From then on, I didn't move unless Harley was upwind. With every ascending circle I'd move twenty feet ahead with Moose at close heel. When I figured the grouse were within Moose's range I stopped and waited for Harley to get into perfect position. I stroked Moose the way I did during the pigeon game. If she would charge ahead and flush the grouse while I stayed right where I was, Harley would get her shot. I was putting a lot of pressure on a pup. I reminded myself not to shout when the grouse flushed. I didn't want Moose to think she had done something wrong.

It seemed to take forever but finally Harley came up, facing the right direction, high, with the wind at her back. "Get 'em up, girl." And Moose took off like a tiny plump pogo stick gone wild. Harley watched her and pumped that much higher.

The first grouse almost lost a tail feather to Moose, who bounced high off the ground with all four feet outstretched, ears spread and jaws snapping. But Moose was the least of that grouse's problems and he knew it. He rocketed up, then seemed to slow as he found Harley, who was already halfway down. The grouse watched Harley as it flew and I knew it planned to try to roll out of the way of her stoop. It is an effective evasion if the falcon is young and dumb, and I was ready to see Harley go for the fake and end up with a couple of feathers and no pitch. But the rollout only works when the falcon slows—even a tiny bit—to grab the grouse. If it flies all the way down, there is no time for fancy rolls and the grouse sustains a serious hit.

That is exactly what happened. Harley didn't go for the deke. She kept her eye on the ball and gave it all she had. The grouse exploded like a pillow hit by a shotgun. It tumbled, tried to right itself, and flew into the ground. Harley pitched up, and from the corner of my eye I saw Moose streaking for the downed grouse.

There was nothing I could do. Moose is a retriever and a downed bird triggers something in a retriever that you must not discourage. She had no way of knowing that, though the grouse was down and dazzled, it wasn't going to let itself get caught by a puppy. The only way that grouse was going to get caught was if Harley was allowed to line up on it and hit it again. But Moose was going to be in the way and there was nothing I could do. I could have yelled to stop her, but she was too young to understand the subtleties of when to flush and when not to. I had to let her screw things up. The grouse sidestepped Moose just as Harley shot overhead. That gave the grouse an upwind flush and he took it. His flight was wobbly but good enough; he left Moose and Harley without a chance.

By the time I'd called Harley into the lure and picked her up, Erney had driven the pickup across the field and climbed out with a huge smile on his face. "Hell of a flight," he said.

"Too bad she didn't catch it," I said. "She deserved it." I slipped Harley's hood on and drew the braces closed. "Maybe I'll try her in the morning."

I woke up before light and barely noticed the watercolor sky. Again I'd dreamed of stoops, Harley growing steadily larger in the lens, pumping vertically down through the air like an avian octopus, but fast. Very, very fast.

Sometime in the night I'd made up my mind to drive down to the hawking ground. It was an hour each way and there seemed to be plenty of grouse locally, but I wanted to give Harley every possible chance to succeed. Her success and mine seemed intertwined.

BLOCK OUT. To put a falcon outdoors on her perch.

I took Harley and all the dogs. In a note, I told Erney to go ahead and block out Little Bird, Dundee, and Alice. I asked him to weigh them and give them a bath. I'd be back to fly them in the afternoon.

A trio of grouse were waiting for us as we pulled into the hawking ground. They ran out onto the dirt road that led along the edge of the wheat and lined out ahead of the pickup. I stopped and backed up until they ducked left into the taller grass a hundred yards ahead. It was the kind of cover they'd hold in and I made myself wait five minutes before I even got out of the pickup. I wasn't exactly sure where they'd be, and I wanted them to put down some scent.

Melville got the call. Once Harley had reached her pitch, I sent him right down the road. A hundred feet from where I'd seen the grouse disappear, Melville spun into the wind. When Harley saw that, she pumped straight into position above him. I moved in to flush, and when the birds came up, Harley met the first one with a thud.

This time there was no cutting the grouse down and pitching up to try to pin it to the ground. This time she simply wadded it up in her talons like a man building a fire with a newspaper. It struggled but to no avail. She set her wings and took it neatly to the earth. I ran to where she held it in the stubble. Only after I was kneeling beside her with Melville peering over my shoulder did I notice that I was breathing hard. My fists were clenched and I had to tell myself to calm down.

We made it back easily in time to fly the other birds. Even though they all flew well, it was something of a chore. I couldn't get over Harley's flight. I wanted to see it again, and again, and again.

The next morning we made the drive to the hawking ground. Harley flew well, but the grouse escaped through a fluke. I found myself crushed with disappointment and fed her only a bite when she came back to the lure. I wanted to fly her again; however, we were experiencing a very warm and windy weather pattern and by ten-thirty the conditions were ideal for losing a falcon. I decided to hold off and fly her again that evening.

We drove back to the ranch for a late lunch. Erney and I waited for the wind to go down but that didn't happen until an hour before dark, at which point there wasn't time to fly all the birds. Erney agreed to fly Little Bird while I looked for a slip at local grouse. Dundee and Alice didn't get flown.

Harley caught another grouse that night. Two days later she caught another one, in a long flat stoop that showed that her confidence was enabling her to catch grouse she could never have caught a month before. It went on like this for two weeks: getting up early, getting back late, spending most of my time driving back and forth to the hawking ground, leaving the other birds for Erney to fly. I told myself that I was doing what I always wanted to do, that I was finally feeling the fulfillment the sport of falconry had always promised. But I was tired and tense, demanding of Harley and the dogs and myself.

Now I know that I was mostly caught up in a numbers game. I had an exceptional bird and it was making me greedy, forgetful of my real purpose, and stupid. Much later, I realized that I had begun to turn the opportunity of a lifetime into a familiar, vulgar dance.

It was the warmest November in memory. There were still meadowlarks and the odd dove in the fields around the ranch. The nights were cool and occasionally there was a rim of ice on the smaller ponds, but few ducks had moved farther south. I was driving a hundred and fifty miles a day to ensure that Harley got at least two good slips a day, and the warm weather was adding to my general frustration. Some days the wind would come up to thirty miles an hour as the sun rose toward its zenith. If it had been cooler, a good falcon could still have been effective on ducks, but with grouse there were just too many variables. I sometimes had to sit out the middle of the day for fear Harley would feel the tug of migration in that unseasonably warm wind. Often, though, we had already caught a grouse by the time the wind came up. Harley's powers increased with each flight. She began to show me things I had never seen before. Everything got bigger, faster, harder.

She caught a grouse that flushed fifty yards from where Mel pointed the main group. When it got up and she started her stoop I groaned because I thought there would be no chance of catching it. The grouse must have thought the same thing or it would have stayed hidden on the ground. But, for a reason I still don't understand, the grouse wasn't able to pull away from her. At the end of her stoop Harley flared and cut right, slashing the grouse across the back. It looked like a glancing blow but the grouse tumbled. My eyes were on the grouse so I don't know how Harley pitched up so fast. Her second stoop came while the grouse was still cartwheeling. She cut it again before it hit the ground. When I cleaned the grouse I found a massive hematoma at the back of its skull.

By then there was no question that Harley was the finest falcon I had ever flown. I reveled in her abilities, but on the few occasions when I called Kris I didn't mention Harley. She was a dream falcon: a high flyer who was absolutely confident in her ability to catch grouse. I didn't think Kris would want to hear about it, and Kris didn't ask.

Harley was one of those birds that always seem to do the right thing. If something odd happened in a flight, she anticipated it. If I was unable to get a grouse up, she did not drift off, she went higher and farther into the wind. She waited until I got the grouse up, and the longer it took, the more likely she was to catch it. She caught them with one foot, she killed them dead in the air, she caught them in cover. And even though I drove her, her manners were perfect. I loved that bird and carried her in the evenings around the yard and house, not because she needed it, but because I wanted her on my fist. After Erney went to bed in his cabin I would sit by the stove with the dogs spread out asleep on the kitchen floor and stroke her breast. I talked to her as if she could understand what I was saying.

My confidence in her was so great by the middle of November that, on a too warm, too windy morning, I put her up over a group of ten grouse I had watched land in a great field of swaying wheat grass. It was an insane thing to do with the wind blowing thirty miles an hour but she had missed a grouse earlier that morning and I didn't want to go home empty-handed. We were on our hawking ground. She'd flown over that field a dozen times before and I really thought there was a good chance she would catch a grouse. But after I pulled the braces of the hood with my teeth and right hand, I hesitated. The hood was open and loose on Harley's head—it needed only to be lifted off. Harley paddled her wings in anticipation. But something told me not to lift the hood.

The ties that bound me to Harley were strong, but the conditions of that day would test any bond. In some ways I wanted that test—I wanted to know if we could be successful in such a wind. But there was ego at work, too. I wanted to be able to say that I'd killed a sharp-tailed grouse with a peregrine against all odds.

When I lifted the hood from her head, the wind took her off the fist and south. Melville ran forward and Harley flipped over him like a harrier. That was not like her, but then she started to go up. The

HARRIER. A marsh hawk, known for its light, low flight.

wind was growing even more intense. Catching a grouse in a wind like that is a nearly impossible feat, but I thought she was up to the task. I moved ahead.

A grouse got up wild and I saw her tip toward it, but she didn't chase. Then grouse were getting up all around me. The slip was going to hell and I tried to find Harley in the sky. But there was nothing but grouse disappearing over the near horizon. In a moment, Melville and I were standing in the middle of the field with nothing in the sky above us but puffy white clouds careering southward at incredible speed.

The warm wind in the grass was eerie as I stood swinging the lure in case she was within sight and not on a grouse. There was no response and although there was still that strange feeling in the air, I welcomed a sense of déjà vu. The only other time she had been out of my sight for that long had been when she had caught that grouse after a three-and-a-half-mile flight. That flight had originated only a half mile from where I stood scanning the horizon with squinting eyes.

Like that first flight, I got no telemetry signal when I returned to the truck. I made my way to all the high spots for a mile in each direction. No signal.

The wind increased. By the time I got to the airport it was blowing forty-five miles per hour. The pilot who flew me the last time was on his way to Denver and no one else would be available for at least another hour. I taped the antenna to the wing strut and waited. The windsock in the middle of the field remained parallel to the ground.

It was almost two o'clock when we popped off the runway. Harley had been missing for about four hours. She could easily be hundreds of miles away, far out of the telemetry's range. We climbed

away from the airport on the same vector we had climbed the last
time she was lost, and I tried to be confident. There was the hope
that the signal would again begin to ping dimly through the static.
There was a hope that she'd be found again as the sun set, just fin-
ishing her grouse. But when we reached altitude there was nothing
but electric crackling in the earphones. We went up another thousand feet, did a slow pylon turn, rose another thousand feet.

With every fruitless turn my insides grew more hollow. She
was nowhere near the hawking grounds. I told the pilot to begin flying a grid that would fan out with the wind. We began the deadening task of searching the five thousand square miles to the southeast.
It's country that includes Badlands National Park and the Pine Ridge
Indian Reservation—all the way to Nebraska. There was a chance
that she was perched on the side of one of the crumbling buttes, but
there was no guarantee that she had even gone that direction.

For hours we continued to transect the southwestern quarter
of South Dakota, eliminating swaths of prairie ten miles wide. With
every passing minute the area where she might be expanded expo-
nentially. More and more, finding her became a matter of luck and
more and more I felt that luck was not with us. She could be any-
where. I finally had to admit that the chances of ever seeing her again
were just about nil. By the time the sun was fully down the airplane
was low on fuel and I was sick with regret.

It was ten o'clock when I came down the ranch driveway.
The light was on in the kitchen and I saw Erney come to the window to see who it was. I dreaded facing him. The night was clear
and the moon was bright. After blowing all day, it was now still. I
fed the dogs and put them in the kennel for the night. The moonlight made angular shadows of the hackbox. I stared at it, thinking

about how Harley had claimed it as hers, how her first flight had started there.

Finally, I went into the house and told Erney that she was gone. It didn't surprise him but it made him quiet. The silence made me focus on the things I'd done wrong. I shouldn't have pushed her so hard. I should have treasured her more. I should have used her as a conduit to a better understanding of her world, not as an amplifier of the values of mine. Erney drank a beer with me, not because he wanted one but because he wanted me to know that he didn't blame me. But I blamed myself. I swore I'd go look for her the next day, though both of us knew it was hopeless.

I had a few more beers that night. I had a glass of whiskey. I lay in my sleeping bag on the deck and looked at the sky. It felt like the stars were watching me. If they were, they were watching Harley too. God only knew where she was, most likely hundreds of miles away. I lost another bird once and he turned up in Abilene, Texas, six days later. Someone saw him hit a glass building when he tried to cut through to catch a pigeon. He was dead when I got the call, but at least I got a call. Lying there that night, looking up at the sky and feeling somehow close to Harley, I knew that I would never hear from her again.

For two days I drove to the hawking ground and swung a lure on the high places. It was silly but I had to do it; I didn't feel like doing anything else. I wallowed in self-recrimination and did a kind of penance on those windy hillsides with the lure sweeping, sweeping,

sweeping the air for hours. At night I drank my whiskey and thought of how things might have been. Sleep came hard. In the mornings, nothing interested me. Erney understood and did the best he could with the other birds.

Finally I gave up going to the hawking ground and just sat in the house. For two days I was completely silent. I didn't make any calls and I let the telephone ring. I was afraid it would be Kris and I didn't want to talk to her.

But on the third day, at lunchtime the phone rang and Erney answered. "Hello?"

He nodded. "Yeah. Right here," and he handed the phone to me.

It wasn't Kris and I was glad. It was Tom Montgomery, from Jackson, Wyoming. He is a photographer/fishing guide friend and we'd been talking for a year about getting together to do some fishing. "I know it's pretty late in the year," he said, "but we're having a real heat wave for November. Why don't you come over and we'll hike into Yellowstone."

I started to decline the invitation: "I don't know . . ."

"I saw a fish up there this summer and I've been meaning to get back. He's a whopper. I just haven't had time until now. We could hike into the river in an hour or so, maybe do a couple of days on the Snake if the weather holds."

Erney was watching me. I knew I'd been making him crazy. A few days driving and fishing might not be a bad idea even if it didn't sound like much fun just then. "When are you thinking?"

"This weather isn't going to last forever. Tomorrow?"

It was like pushing a rock uphill. "I suppose. I kind of need to get out of here."

"Fantastic. Wait until you see Bruno."

"Bruno?"

"The fish," Tom said. "I've been thinking about him all fall."

It took about two minutes to pack: sleeping bag, fishing stuff, extra pants, shirt, and underwear. Suddenly I wanted to get away from the ranch as soon as I could. It was a full day's drive to Jackson and that sounded good, not because it was through some of the most magnificent country in the world but because I'd be alone and on the move. I've always thought that whoever said you can't run away from your troubles simply wasn't very fast.

I was rolling by twelve-thirty—through the northwest corner of the Black Hills, just south of Devil's Tower, past Gillette, under the shadow of the Big Horns. I raced to the top and caught another hour of sunlight on the other side of the divide. I ran through Greybull, Thermopolis, and up the Wind Canyon like I was driving a getaway car. Right at Riverton, over Togowotee, and into Jackson Hole. I got to the town of Jackson at eleven o'clock. Ten and a half hours of driving didn't seem like enough. I thought about going right up over Teton Pass and into Idaho but Tom was waiting and besides, I had to stop somewhere.

Tom and I drank a couple of beers and I crashed on the couch. *Heart of Darkness* was on the coffee table and I read a few pages before falling into an intermittent sleep. Each time I slid back to consciousness I was wondering something different. Where was Harley? of course. But also things like, Why Conrad's choice of narrator? Was Little Darryl still alive? Were there Blue-Winged Olives in my fishing vest?

I woke, exhausted, to Tom building coffee in the kitchen. He's a fishing, skiing, photography bum, a bachelor, educated in England, who smokes good cigars when he can get them and drinks good whiskey when he sells a picture. He's also an equipment nut and his house is a bazaar of art, reels, rods, and good books. He's good company and can talk about just about anything. That morning he mostly wanted to talk about Bruno.

In my state of mind I didn't much care about a particular fish. As we made our way up to the park, the details of Tom's first encounter did get my attention. Everybody says, "It's the biggest fish I ever saw," and it's never really true. But it's an indicator, and Tom has seen some really big fish. He's fished and guided around the world: Alaska, New Zealand, Argentina, all over the West. When Tom says, "It's the biggest fish I ever saw," you've got to take notice.

I was still listless. I'd sailed too close to the wind and the canvas that made me go was slack. I was only there because I didn't want to be anyplace else. Not even the hike into Yellowstone perked me up. When we got to the river and I saw how rich and challenging it was, there was no real excitement in me to catch a fish.

We pulled on our waders and I tagged along as Tom made his way upstream to Bruno's lair. Twice he waved me down like a lieutenant leading a squad of infantrymen. He made a couple of sneaks on oxbows that he thought might be the place, but it wasn't until the third try that he came hurrying back with an astounded grin on his face. "That's it," he said. "He's there. He's feeding." I started forward to have a look and Tom jerked me to the ground: "Stay low, for God's sake!"

I approached the water like a cat and parted the grass to see a pool at the mouth of a tiny inlet that trickled water from somewhere up a grassy drainage. The light was good but even with polarized lenses I couldn't see anything. Then a pair of lips sipped the surface. I can't tell the size of a fish from its lips but it told me exactly where to concentrate my gaze. I looked deep, deep, deeper and finally I could discern shapes on the bottom. There were two fish there, both nice size, lying three feet to either side of a log. Then the log rose up and sipped another fly from the surface.

"Jesus Christ." It was involuntary and not loud enough to scare the fish, but Tom had me by the ankle and was pulling me back. "Shhh," he was saying. "Shhh, shhh."

We sat in the reed-grass and I shook my head as he smiled moronically. Our packs formed the edge of Tom's little base camp. His camera gear was piled at the perimeter. A row of fly boxes was laid out on one of the packs and Tom was absently testing tippet material as he spoke. "Nice rainbow, huh?"

"He's got to be thirty inches."

"I figure he's the biggest rainbow in the Yellowstone ecosystem."

I didn't ask how he figured that because, even with no data, I believed him. "What's he eating?"

"Something very small." He was digging into a pile of tiny gray midge imitations. "I'm thinking eighteens." He concentrated on tying tippet onto the leader, then started attaching the fly. My rod was still in the case and I saw it dawn on Tom that he should offer Bruno to me.

"No, no," I said. "This is your deal. I'm going to watch." This was a tough fish. He had to be smart to be that big. He'd chosen a feeding lie with gin-clear water that would amplify any disturbance on the surface. There was almost no good approach. This was definitely a job for someone with Tom's skills. I watched closely as he assumed the New Zealand creep position with his fly rod held up and back to keep the line from fouling in the grass. He sank to his belly and slithered through the flora like a salamander.

There was one place where I could safely see Tom and the inlet that held Bruno. It was a hundred and fifty feet away, so I couldn't actually see the fish. But every now and then the flat surface snapped as he sipped another bug from the current created by the little drainage. The river behind the fish was wide and featureless and I imagined what it would be like to fight him in a stretch like that. He'd be back and forth across that stream like a handball shot from a cannon. Backing would be showing before Tom could struggle to his feet. Being a rainbow, Bruno would probably be airborne half the time. If he ran downstream Tom would have to do a ten-second hundred in waders to have a chance of keeping him on.

It took Tom ten minutes to get into position. The bank was steep, so he had to get fairly close to keep the line out of the grass. He lay on his side, stripped thirty feet of line, and took a couple of false casts. Something wasn't right. He brought the line in and crawled three feet to his left. Finally he sent a lovely loop out to the very mouth of the trickle that was bringing the bugs to Bruno. He mended twice with tiny flips of the rod tip and the fly started its dead drift toward the sweet spot. Just before it got there, Bruno came up and snarfed a natural. The imitation bounced over the wake of the rise and on past Bruno's window. Tom let the fly float all the way into the main current before he began his cautious retrieve. He cast again but not far enough, and the fly missed Bruno by six inches. But Tom still let it float fifteen feet beyond the fish before he started to retrieve.

In the next forty-five minutes Tom made eight perfect casts, but Bruno wasn't buying. He was still sipping naturals so we crawled back to the base camp to confer. "I can't tell what he's eating," Tom said.

"How about a surprise?" I said. "Throw a hopper at him."

"They've been dead for six weeks."

"He's eaten a million of them."

Tom shrugged. "I'll try it."

The hopper didn't work either. I marveled at Tom's casts. He was rolling them out forty feet from a prone position. The fly was coming over within five inches of where it hit the time before and there was a nifty little reach at the end that gave him just enough slack to get to Bruno with no hint of drag. The fact that Bruno wasn't taking the fly didn't matter. On every cast I was convinced that he might.

We ate lunch and decided that it had to be emergers that Bruno craved. Tom tried three patterns and only once did he even get a look. "But he looked," Tom said as he carefully trimmed the tail of a tiny drab fly with his clippers. "Maybe we just need a little tweak." He took another sixteenth of an inch off the fly's tail. "You want a shot at him?"

"No."

I really didn't. I was engrossed in watching Tom. He was crazed and it was wonderful. He was completely focused and his senses were fine-tuned. He went to wet flies. I watched him tie on a pheasant tail and a nearly microscopic weight. I watched him creep back and forth into position. I watched that gentle cast and the fly touch the water softer than a real insect would. I watched him all day long, but I never saw him hook Bruno.

At nightfall Bruno was still there, undisturbed, and while hiking out, that made me smile. I was chuckling in the car on the way back to Tom's house. By the time we got to where we could buy a six-pack we were both giddy with the day. We drank and drove and I was reminded of Kris. Drinking beer and driving is one of our favorite pastimes. She claims it's legal if you're listening to the right kind of music. I slipped Ray Charles into the tape player and lit a Cuban cigar. My rod had never come out of the case but I knew that day would go down as one of the best. I collapsed onto Tom's couch and didn't twitch until seven the next morning.

When I woke up I knew I had to get back to the ranch. I left Tom a note saying I'd have to pass on fishing the Snake; I had something to do at home. I thanked him for the great day in Yellowstone.

A dark cloud bank chased me across northern Wyoming, but I didn't let it bother me. I stopped to wet a line in Ten Sleep Creek on the west side of the Big Horns, and spent the night in the canyon below a huge cliff where I'm sure peregrines will be nesting soon. It was cold at that elevation and the cloud bank caught up in the night. It moved through in the darkness, leaving only a trace of snow behind to trap the first rays of morning sunlight. On the way down the east side of the Big Horns, steam rose from the asphalt and mule deer stood on the shoulders. I could see for a hundred miles.

As soon as I pulled into the ranch yard I went to the mews and slowly opened the door. I might have harbored a tiny hope that Harley would be there, but of course she wasn't. The sunlight cut across the screen perch and Alice, Little Bird, and Dundee turned their heads like a dance troupe about to begin its routine. I stepped up to each one, stroked their breasts, and made my apologies. Little Bird bit me, but not hard.

I carried them to the weathering yard and blocked them in the crisp sunlight. It was cool, but warm enough to put out a bath for each. They jumped right in and shimmied down into the water like old ladies donning girdles. I watched until they were back on their perches, draped like drying socks and beginning to preen. Then Erney came out of the house with Spud and Melville stretching and yawning at his heels. Moose flew off the deck, picked up a stick, and started running around the house. Erney hobbled up to where I stood watching the birds and handed me a cup of coffee. He didn't say a word until we had both taken a sip. "Bunch of doves in that milo down by Chet's."

"Doves? Got to be too late for doves."

He shrugged. "Kind of odd, but they must have their reasons. And a giant flock of gadwalls and wigeons on Johnson's Big Pond."

I nodded. "You been out and about."

"A guy's got to try and keep up," he said. "You never can tell."

We sipped more coffee and watched the birds preen in the warm sunlight. I'd forgotten how I love to watch them run their beaks down every flight feather, how the tail feathers bend as they finish their sweep, the way the birds' eyes go nearly shut with pleasure. Spud and Melville came and sat beside us. "Catch any fish?" Erney asked.

I shook my head. "No."

He nodded and let Moose whiz past a couple of times. "Gonna be a great day to fly birds."

The temperature was around thirty degrees and the wind was out of the north at less than ten. "Yeah," I said. "Could be real good."

And it was. The weather was holding the ducks, and doves, and meadowlarks, and white-crowned sparrows against the north slope of the Black Hills. I called Kris. She told me that Little Darryl's hair was growing back and it had snowed four inches the night before. She said the humidity made the air feel colder than it was. I told her that I'd be with her soon.

For the next week winter remained stalled somewhere in Canada and I felt reprieved. I walked the fields with Alice for hours. I concentrated on the colors at the base of the grass, the subtle smells in the air, the sky. I stretched my legs and Alice stretched her wings. We must have started every little bird for miles. We soaked up the changing season and we took our time.

In the afternoons Little Bird was put up over ducks or partridge points and she flew like a spirit, soaring high above and stooping like a jagged check mark. Moose leaped headlong into the icy duck ponds and swam after the ducks as if they were her favorite slipper. In the last light of the days I flew Dundee to the lure in the front yard. He loved it, stooping hard and pitching up vertically on the other side. He wore me out, thirty, forty, fifty stoops without opening his beak. He never set his wings.

Erney and I ate what Little Bird caught. We roasted the birds in the cold night and breathed in the rich smells. We ate with our hands, laughed, and relived every flight in the glow of the woodstove. The bath pans froze thicker every night and we knew autumn was in South Dakota on borrowed time. I was, too.

When the first tough blast of winter finally came, it came with an attitude. Zero degrees. Wind. The ponds were frozen in hours, the seed-eating birds were sent streaking for the Gulf. I awoke to a different world and instantly my thoughts turned to Kris. I'd had my autumn. It was time to catch up with the rest of life.

The birds all got triple rations when they went into their molting chambers. The jesses and bewits were set to soak in neatsfoot oil. The hoods and bells were hung on the rack, the gloves and leashes oiled and put away. I packed my computer, a hundred books, and a little bag of clothes in the pickup. Spud and Melville got an extra blanket in their kennels in the truck bed.

On a blustery Monday morning in late November we set off for New Hampshire, leaving Erney to wrestle the winter assisted only by Moose, elevated to "inside dog"—Queen Bitch of the ranch. I didn't worry about them. I worried a little about me, tracking two thousand miles across the middle of America, and at first I moved with a twinge of regret. But once we crossed the midway mark, somewhere in Illinois, perhaps, the prairie seemed to fade and the magnetism of the earth switched. I felt myself being pulled toward Kris. Stronger in Indiana and Ohio, and stronger still on the New York Thruway. By the time we reached Vermont the cruise control was set at seventy-five and I only slowed down for policemen and school crossings.

Post-
Season

*I*t was the now famous winter of 1996. By Christmas, a foot of snow covered the little yellow house, the stone fence, and the grouse woods beyond. Little Darryl's cancer went into remission and he went home, at least for a while. Kris continued to work all day in the critical care unit at Dartmouth-Hitchcock Hospital. Three nights a week she stayed in the unit, adjusting the blood gases of postoperative patients and threading monitoring lines into faulty hearts. We spent the other four nights each week together, a fire in the fireplace, something rich simmering on the stove, not bothering to say too much. I set up the word processor on a card table in the living room and went back to work. Twice a day, I walked Spud and Mel in the woods behind the house.

Winter thickened and the snow forced me to run the dogs on skis. Pernicious little politicians shut the government down in January, then three more feet of snow shut it down for real. Spud was even slower than he'd been the month before but both dogs plunged off the trail, through deep snow, as long as they could, running the ski tracks when they needed a rest. We all missed the prairie; I dreamed of it almost every night. I came to think of that part of our lives as an enormous volume of light, fluffy air, a million cubic miles, filled birds, and grass, and sunlight. I imagined that part of our lives on the other end of a two-thousand-mile-long arm. At our end of the arm were the little yellow New Hampshire house and four souls—two canine and two human.

In February, the pain in Erney's leg became too much and he embarked on a series of operations that would make him more mobile. Perhaps I should have gone back to take care of the ranch while he was disabled, but I wanted to stay with Kris. My brother Scott volunteered to nurse Erney. When I saw that the temperature on the plains had dipped to thirty-five below, I called them. Sure, no problem, they said. The birds were fine. On the coldest night the top of the stovepipe had frosted over and the house filled with smoke. The windchill was fifty-five below so they didn't feel much like getting up on the dark and slippery roof to open it. They popped the stovepipe cap off with a shotgun blast and the stove started drawing again, no problem. Their story made me miss the ranch, but I didn't want to go back. I felt torn between where I belonged and to whom I belonged until one white puffy morning, skiing with the dogs. Another foot of snow had fallen during the night and to step off the skis meant going in up to my thighs. Spud and Mel struggled ahead of me, up to their bellies in the powder. I didn't notice that they had stopped until I nearly skied over them. I wasn't sure what they were doing. They stood still, but their tails wagged slowly. They tilted their heads toward the thick cushion of snow just under their noses. We stood like that for probably a minute, then I poked the snow in front of Spud with a ski pole. A ruffed grouse flew up through the snow and into the air without missing a wing beat. Then a second one popped up, then two more. Another. And another. Both dogs looked at me and I spoke for us all: "Wow."

And that night I lay in bed thinking how thankful I was that the dogs had led me to those grouse. Seeing them explode from the snow was a sight I would never have witnessed without them. As usual, they had been my guides. Then, for a long time, I thought of some of the sights and experiences that falconry had led me to, how an association with wild things has a way of shining an unexpected brilliant light into the darkest crevices of our lives.

I wanted to think that I would have come to New Hampshire in November as I'd promised whether I'd lost Harley or not. I wanted to believe I could resist the siren's song, that perhaps I'd lost Harley on purpose. But lying there in our bed that night I couldn't say for sure.

I felt Spud and Melville jump onto the bed and begin to search for the perfect place to lie down. With Kris asleep beside me I closed my eyes and saw those millions of cubic miles of air over the prairie. It was a lattice of life from dirt to stooping falcons. It was palpable and had great weight. The dogs settled on each side of us and rolled the covers under them. The effect was to shrink-wrap Kris and me together. The four of us there on that bed were tiny compared to the domain of the falcons. But we had gravity too. Every time a dog moved we came closer together and our density increased. I remembered what Kris had said about the equinox being a time of balance. Now I was confident that the four of us could keep stable all that life at the other end of the arm in South Dakota if we remained close. We could counter the magnitude of anything if we lay close to the fulcrum; we could find a balance if we pushed tight together and stayed that way.

Glossary

A complete lexicon of hunting terms would make an interesting book in itself. The etymology of falconry terms is fascinating. Unfortunately, there is no room for that here. A short list of a few of the odd and otherwise useless words found in the text will have to do.

accipiter. A genus of raptor with short wings and a long tail, known for short bursts of speed. Accipiters are the true hawks, represented in North America by the sharp-shinned hawk, Cooper's hawk, and goshawk.

air-washed. The loss of scent that game birds undergo by flying. Such birds are difficult for dogs to scent immediately after the flight.

back. The action of a dog when it stops behind another dog that is on point. Generally, both dogs can scent the game.

bate. To fly from the fist or a perch and be brought up short by the leash. This is to be avoided.

bell. The act of attaching a bell to a falcon or hawk's leg.

belton. A color phase of dog, usually an English setter, in which the black or orange is distributed in very small spots over a coat of white.

bewit. The leather strap that holds an accessory (bell, name tag, radio transmitter) to the leg of a falcon or a hawk.

biddable. Trainable, willing to obey.

bind. To seize quarry in the air.

block. A cylinder, usually of laminated wood, staked to the ground and used by falcons as a perch while weathering.

block out. To put a falcon outdoors on her perch.

brace. One of two leather straps that open and close a hood; the act of closing a hood.

bracelet. Usually leather straps wrapped around the legs of a falcon or a hawk and secured with a grommet. The jesses are threaded through the grommet.

broke. Description of a completely trained pointing dog. A broke dog does not chase game but stands steady when birds are flushed and shot.

buteo. A genus of bird of prey with long, broad wings and short wide tails. Buteos are more sluggish than falcons or accipiters but some are suited for falconry, especially the red-tailed hawk.

cadge. A wooden frame perch used to carry falcons and hawks.

call off. To call a hawk to the fist or a falcon to the lure for food.

carry. This term has two meanings in falconry. One is to walk with a falcon or hawk on the fist, usually as part of the training process. The second meaning refers to a vice of falcons or hawks who fly away from the falconer "carrying" quarry they have caught.

cast. A pair of falcons flown together. Also, to hold a falcon or hawk, as when jesses and bells are being attached. Also, to launch a bird into the air from the fist; to cast off.

cere. The soft skin at the base of the beak, usually yellow in adult birds of prey and a bluish green in immatures.

chip. A soft vocalization of a friendly and contented falcon.

clutch. A group of eggs or young birds, usually from a single nesting effort of a pair of adults.

Conservation Reserve Program (CRP). The Department of Agriculture program that promotes seeding marginal farmland back to grass. The CRP is responsible for a huge increase in wildlife populations.

cover. An area that is likely to hold birds, usually woodcock or ruffed grouse. Sometimes called covert.

creance. A long, strong string used to ensure that a falcon or hawk will not fly away in the initial stages of training.

crop. The membranous pouch in the gullet of a bird where food is stored before it is digested.

deck feathers. The middle two feathers in a bird's tail.

eechip. A sharp, solicitous vocalization of a falcon, usually around the nest, which indicates contentment. It is often used as a greeting.

enter. To introduce a falcon or hawk to its intended quarry.

eyas. A falcon or hawk in its first few months of life; a falcon whose training began as a chick.

falcon. Purists follow the ancients' lead and use the term falcon to refer only to the female peregrine falcon. But it also can mean a female of any species of falcon. A still more general usage applies to any of the long-winged birds of prey, male or female, as opposed to the short-winged hawks.

feak. A stropping action used by birds to clean their beaks on a perch or the glove.

foot. To strike or grab with a foot. Some falcons and hawks are much better than others with their feet.

game hawk. This term does not usually refer to hawks at all but to a falcon trained to catch game birds from a pitch.

hack. To release falcons or hawks into the wild temporarily to allow them to develop their powers of flight and emotional maturity more naturally; to release into the wild permanently.

hackbox. The home of hack falcons or hawks in the week before release and the place where they are fed until they are taken up for training.

hard penned. The culmination of feather growth, when the feather reaches full length and the nourishing blood inside the quill dries, leaving the feather hard and complete.

harrier. A marsh hawk, known for its light, low flight.

hawk. Strictly speaking these are accipiters—short-winged hawks—but the term can also refer to buteos and even falcons used in the sport of falconry.

honor. The action of a dog when it freezes upon seeing another dog on point. Usually only the first dog scents the birds.

hood. The sometimes exquisitely made leather cap that covers a falcon's head and eyes. Used to keep the falcon calm and safe before flying or in potentially frightening situations; the act of putting the hood on the falcon.

hup. Traditional command used for hunting dogs; to lie down.

intermew. To keep a bird of prey through a molt.

jess. The leather strap between the bracelets and the swivel.

kakking. A noise made by excited falcons.

leash. Usually a leather strap about three feet in length and one half inch wide with a "button" on the end. This allows the swivel to turn while the other end of the leash is tied to the perch.

lure. The usually leather pouch garnished with meat and swung to call a falcon to the falconer. Falcons are fed **on the lure.**

make. To successfully encourage a falcon to kill.

make in. To approach a trained bird of prey on its kill.

man. To tame by prolonged and intimate exposure to people and the human world.

mandible. Either segment of a bird's beak.

mantle. A hunched, drooped wing posture of falcons and hawks. Often used to protect a kill or the lure. Also a comfort movement in birds, to stretch a wing and leg on the same side at the same time.

mar-hawk. A bird that has been spoiled in some way.

mews. The place where falcons and hawks are housed.

molt. A bird's annual change of feathers, usually in the spring and summer.

noose carpet. A rectangle of woven wire to which monofilament loops are tied in such a way that, when food is placed under the wire, the nooses will entangle the feet of a falcon or hawk trying to get the food.

passage. The trip of a migrating bird. A term describing a migrating bird, i.e., a passage falcon.

pitch. The height of a falcon as she waits on.

pitch up. To shoot back up after a stoop; a hunting maneuver that readies the falcon for a second stoop.

quarry. The particular game pursued by a falcon or hawk.

raptor. Any bird of prey.

recall pen. A secure wire cage built so that game birds can get into it but cannot get out unless released by a person.

reclaim. The term has come to mean the retraining of an intermewed falcon or hawk but used to refer to the training of any class of falcon or hawk.

refuse. To pass up the opportunity to chase game.

ring up. To ascend, usually by circling and usually in an effort to get above another bird.

rouse. To align the feathers by shaking the entire body, as a dog would dry itself.

screen perch. A long perch used to keep falcons, and occasionally hawks, at night. A cloth screen hangs below the perch so the bird cannot go under and get tangled. These perches are not safe unless the birds are healthy and used to them.

slip. A chance to catch quarry.

soar. The nearly effortless flight of a falcon or hawk achieved by the use of air currents. Once the technique is mastered, birds can stay up very high for hours with only occasional wing flapping.

stoop. A falcon's dive from a height—sometimes a considerable height. There are a thousand different configurations of stoops and watching a good one unfold is arguably the most exciting part of game hawking.

strike. To take off a falcon's hood. Also the first bay of a hound when it finds game.

swivel. The necessary metal connector between the jesses and the leash that rotates and keeps everything from twisting and endangering the trained falcon or hawk.

take up. To begin the training of an intermewed or hacked falcon or hawk. Also, to first get a bird on the fist.

tiercel. The male peregrine falcon; the male of any species of falcon.

tiring. A tough piece of food given to a falcon or hawk. A tiring is usually given while the bird is on the fist to prolong the positive association with the falconer.

wait on. To go to a height above the falconer and dogs and stay there until the game is flushed.

wake. The training method used to keep a falcon or hawk awake and in constant contact with the falconer until it relaxes. Waking shortens the training process and greatly eases the total stress on the bird.

warble. The comfort movement of falcons when they lean forward and stretch both wings over their backs, usually without spreading the wings.

way of going. The quality of a dog's gait; the way he carries himself.

weather. To put a falcon or hawk outside on a perch to enjoy the elements of fresh air, sunshine, and even light rain. Falcons and hawks seem to fly better if they have been weathered.

weathering yard. An area where falcons and hawks are weathered. Federal regulations rightly dictate that a weathering yard should be a wire enclosure with a windbreak to ensure that the birds are safe from predators and protected from severe weather.

wed. To be intent on a certain quarry to the exclusion of all other quarry.

whoa. Traditional command used for hunting dogs; to stop.

yarak. A state of high physical and mental readiness in hawks that stimulates them to high performance when hunting.